Quit Your Job, Enjoy Your Work

Quit Your Job, Enjoy Your Work

~

Making Your Workplace More Enjoyable

Garth S. Johns

OPEN BOOK
EDITIONS
A Berrett–Koehler Partner

Quit Your Job, Enjoy Your Work
Making Your Workplace More Enjoyable

iUniverse books may be ordered through booksellers or by contacting:

iUniverse
1663 Liberty Drive
Bloomington, IN 47403
www.iuniverse.com
1-800-Authors (1-800-288-4677)

ISBN: 978-1-4759-2716-0 (sc)
ISBN: 978-1-4759-2718-4 (hc)
ISBN: 978-1-4759-2717-7 (e)

Library of Congress Control Number: 2012908753

Printed in the United States of America

iUniverse rev. date: 07/09/2012

Contents

Acknowledgments

When I first set out on the journey that was to become *Quit Your Job, Enjoy Your Work*, my intent was to create something that readers would not have to struggle to read. Rather, I wanted them to enjoy and, most important, benefit from the messages contained therein. I hope I have achieved that goal.

Certainly, it would never have been possible without the significant contributions of many people. The entire team at iUniverse has both pushed me and encouraged me. While the process has, at times, been frustrating, it has also resulted in a far better product than I would have otherwise created. I am eternally grateful to all their folks for their outstanding guidance. They always had such a nice way of telling me, on occasion, that I was barking up the wrong tree, and when I was, they were always ready to offer valid suggestions for improvements.

My colleagues with the Day of Hope and Leadership served as a huge inspiration for me, just by being there. My good friend Reverend Doug Schneider was always ready, willing, and able to offer ideas, thoughts, and suggestions to me. In addition to our many lunches to discuss content and approach, he also stayed in touch, even when God called him to suffer in places like Hawaii.

To Dan, Denise, Todd, Joe, and all the others on the Day of Hope team, thank you for being there. It was most sincerely appreciated.

Also, for their input and suggestions, I need to recognize Hugh Drouin, Dave Sarookanian, Dan Carnegie, Marty Epp, Barb Baynham, Susie Collins, Bob Merry, and Don Wouters. Your contributions are also sincerely appreciated.

My family is always a source of inspiration to me. Julie, Chad, Andrea, Doug, Meredith, Heather, and Phil all deserve a big thank-you.

Finally, the person who I have used for 37 years as my chief confidante, sounding board, coach, and mentor is my wife, Debi. I could not have done it without you, without your love, and without your friendship. Love always.

There are likely countless others I should also thank. If I have forgotten you, I extend my humblest apologies.

Last, but not least, I recognized the contributions made in my first book by Sadie, the dog. She has now gone on to greener pastures, but she has been replaced by Shelley, who, like Sadie, always listened to my ideas for the book during our daily walks and never once argued or told me I was wrong.

My sincerest thanks are extended to all.

Introduction

Let's be honest. Most of us will have neither the privilege nor the pleasure of being born into a life of luxury. Nor will we become independently wealthy by winning the next big lottery. Notwithstanding the fact that we are unlikely to strike it rich, it remains the case that, in North America at least, we generally hope to enjoy a standard of living that allows us to exist comfortably in our own home, have at least one vehicle, and perhaps enjoy an annual vacation as well as a few other comforts of life. I appreciate that not everyone is quite that lucky. For many, simple survival becomes the sole purpose for getting out of bed every day. However, if we can accept that most of us will continue to aim for a decent living, it also means that we will need to work full time for approximately 40 years of our lives.

In 1974, I began my own version of those 40 years of working. Though I have never won any lotteries, I have been fortunate enough to have been employed full time as a senior administrator or in my own consulting business, throughout that entire period of time. In addition to being in senior HR roles for the bulk of my work life, I have also been blessed with the necessary financial and moral support of my employers and my family, which has allowed me to continue my education. I finished my MBA and became certified in fields such as coaching, organizational development, and conflict management. That education, together with a continuous desire to better understand the nature of leadership, led to my first book, *Common Sense Leadership*, and it continues to drive me to complete what I hope will be my legacy, which is this book. I want to contribute something that will ultimately lead to an improvement in the quality of our workplaces and in our enjoyment of work generally.

For the most part, my time has been spent in human resources roles, and that has given me ample opportunity to observe or listen to far too many employees who have hated coming to work each day or have been counting down the days until retirement. The views that I am sharing in these pages are based on my own learning and anecdotal evidence, accumulated over 40 years and hundreds of exit interviews. I hope that I can pass on what I have learned to you, the reader, so that we can make the world a little bit better.

The last time I checked, although there are those in the world who would argue with this, we are only on the face of this earth once. Because we are obliged to work for such a huge part of that one life, it seems an awful waste of 40 years to not enjoy what we do for a living. Later, in discussing "Theory Y," I note that work should be as natural as play for each of us, and therefore it is something that most of us should enjoy far more than we do. Perhaps our approach to work is in dire need of change.

The really good news is that the work world that was evident in 1900 has mostly disappeared. Generally, we work fewer hours and in better conditions. However, there is still much to do.

It is important to take a moment to reflect on some current social realities, which, in turn, present challenges for us in the new world of work. In the Western world, we are seeing a rise in divorce rates and single-parent families. Additionally, the average family size continues to shrink. Many North American families are simply not replacing themselves, and therefore any labor force growth must, by necessity, come from the ranks of immigrants to the United States and Canada. In most jurisdictions, mandatory retirement has now disappeared, and for the first time in our history, we have four generations in the workplace at the same time. As a result of these factors and others, we have an increasingly diverse population as well as an increasingly diverse and demanding workforce. This has significant implications for how we are managing and leading in our organizations.

Quit Your Job, Enjoy Your Work is intended to be a guide for organizational managers and leaders and even staff who want to simply understand their workplace a little bit better or who aspire to future roles in management. My desire is that, by reading this, they will take the knowledge contained herein and apply it to their own unique situations. The ultimate result will be a better work world for all.

In *Common Sense Leadership*, I laid out 10 ways to become a better leader. This time, my interest is to help create a new workplace where people may actually enjoy attending on most days. If they enjoy their work, there will be less stress, less turnover, less absenteeism, reduced costs of operation, and most important, a happy and healthy workforce.

The book examines three key areas of concern: *leadership, culture*, and *management practices*.

Leadership
Managers are expected to manage. Therefore, they need to plan, organize, implement, delegate, control, and measure, but they must also be leaders. As leaders they are expected to inspire their staff to greater levels of achievement. However, sometimes, we are unsure what great leaders actually look like. Where do they come from, and why do some succeed where others fail? What skills and approaches can you develop to become a better leader?

In addition to a broad-based discussion of leadership practices, I also consider the nature and value of servant leadership and emotional intelligence. Managers who are interested in creating a positive work environment need to better understand both of these contemporary approaches to leadership.

Culture

Every organization, regardless of the size or industry, has a unique personality, one that evolves over time. While the culture may not be able to change overnight, I submit that by focusing on a few key areas, the culture of any organization can become more positive and certainly more enjoyable for all staff. To that end, there are chapters dedicated to culture, work/life balance, having fun at work, the importance of being civil to others, and the need for ethics and integrity.

Management Practices

While leadership and organizational culture are more focused on the big picture, I also wish to meet the needs of the manager and his or her department. One of the greatest shortcomings of so many that I have worked with over the years is their discomfort in dealing with conflict, with change, and with the transition from managing staff to coaching people. These topics are also addressed, as is a consideration of alternative work arrangements.

I hope the information contained in this book is practical and useful. Most importantly, I hope that it leads to improvements in the quality of work life for everybody.

Chapter 1:

Elements of Effective Leadership

Quick, who is the most influential leader in all of our lives? For those of you who suggest Gandhi, Obama, Churchill, Mother Teresa, or other significant political or social figures, you may be mistaken. Even those of you who may have placed my name in this list (thanks, by the way) may be slightly misguided. These are the names that regularly arise together with organizational directors, sports heroes, and miscellaneous others in numerous research studies that have been undertaken over the last year or two. (All right, it was more like a show of hands during my various workshops and presentations given in that time, and I know it's not very scientific, but ...) Without much doubt, most of those whose names were put forward as great leaders (with the exception of mine) had the potential to inspire great numbers of people through good times and bad. What incredible influence they have carried.

However, I would respectfully submit that the most influential leaders for most of us are our own mothers and/or fathers. After all, they are the ones who, for the first 20 or so years of our lives, were in the driver's seats in terms of inspiring us to greater heights—or not! Mothers and fathers as leaders? Why not say the same about soccer coaches? What about teachers? Union executives? Service club presidents?

One of my key premises when writing *Common Sense Leadership* is that everyone can lead and you don't need a title to do so. After all, leadership is defined not by our titles but by our actions. My own definition of a leader is simply "one who inspires others to achieve greater personal heights or higher levels of performance."(1)

Our mothers and fathers have unfortunately often been relegated to the status of being "just Mom," just as a receptionist I recently spoke with was, in her words, "Just a receptionist." However, parents, for most of us, have been held in a special place in all our hearts, and they have had such a huge impact on our lives that it is high time they were recognized as leaders. By the way, I appreciate and respect that in today's world, there are so many others who serve as primary caregivers; my terms *mother* and *father* should be taken to include others as well. Certainly, they can be the most inspiring people for each and every one of us. They can help us to achieve greater personal heights, and they teach us about ethics, values, and principles.

However, once we get to the workplace, others take over. Could it be that the life lessons taught by Mom and Dad carry over to the workplace? I believe the answer is yes and that the practices and principles that need to be promoted at work are often developed, learned, and encouraged at home as well. Leadership is integral to providing a culture and management style that fosters a healthy, productive, and even fun workplace. We are all leaders in some sense, regardless of whether we hold the title. Learning about what makes leadership effective will improve the workplace and the world we live in.

A few years ago, I began the journey that was to become my first book, *Common Sense Leadership.* The intent at that time was to try to convince readers that all of us have a role to play as leaders. However, the more I have researched the topic of leadership and the more I read about it and spoke with staff and organizations about it, the more I came to appreciate something so simple and yet so profound. Work is important, but work is only a part of the totality of our lives, and work can be enjoyable. Yes, we can even have fun there. If I achieve nothing else in my life, I hope to be able to contribute, through this book and my everyday efforts, to the creation of a work life where it is okay to be happy. A workplace where staff aren't regularly looking over their shoulders, fearful of colleagues, bosses, and others. A workplace where one does not put work ahead of family, friends, personal health, and one's own spiritual wellbeing. Perhaps it is time to quit our jobs and start to enjoy our work. Effective leadership is part of how we achieve that.

However, despite our best efforts as leaders, there are challenges to achieving a healthy, fun workplace. In his book, *Coming to Our Senses: Reclaiming the Dignity of Organization Life,* Ron Knowles noted, "Organization life is plagued with serious contradictions. They are well known to anyone who spends time in businesses, government departments, or not-for-profit agencies ... The biggest contradiction is the contrast between the fast-moving, customer centered, efficient organizations, which have emerged from the recent era of radical transformation and the human angst and despair which seem almost universal in those same organizations."(2) Examples of these contradictions are found everywhere and in far too many organizations:

- When we recruit new staff, we tell them how great we are. We tell them we are team oriented, progressive, supportive, and concerned about them as individuals. When they leave, they tell us at exit interviews how demoralized they were, how we didn't care about developing them, how negative the environment was, and how poor our management practices have been. While this isn't the universal experience, it is more prevalent than we care to admit.
- We crave outstanding leadership but so often practise something totally different.
- We know how to resolve conflicts through third-party interventions, but we have no idea how to make staff "play nice

in the sandbox" together, promote effective conflict resolution, or otherwise manage conflict in a positive, proactive, and productive fashion.

- We talk about our people and note how important they are in our missions, visions, and values, but how often do we expect them to be available to us on a 24/7 basis (especially those who are not paid for overtime)? Why do many managers insist on playing favourites? Why do we so often fail to ask for or respect the opinions of our staff? Why do we refuse to take advantage of their collective wisdom?
- We know change is inevitable, and we know that the rate of change is ever increasing. And yet we continue to resist it in so many ways.
- We preach integrity, but a "what's in it for me?" attitude often prevails.
- We continue, as leaders, to demand that staff serve us, when we in fact need to learn to serve them. We need to make them better leaders in their own right.
- We say that we are here to serve and care for the customer but too often we seem to be only concerned that they pay the bill.

By the way, in case you think I forgot them, I believe that parents know a thing or two about over-promising and under-delivering, about conflict management, about working overtime, change management, integrity, listening to their charges, etc. We just never think of them that way.

My point is that this sort of thing happens far too often and in this changing world we work in, inconsistencies between messages given to potential staff and the reality of our workplaces cannot continue to be so diametrically opposed. We are entering a period of intense competition for limited human resources. We all want to proclaim ourselves as "employers of choice," but the only way we can wear that label with pride is by walking the talk, and that starts with understanding what a good leader is and how leadership impacts the corporate culture and management of the employees.

Words Leaders Live By

While I encourage managers to be more than a person simply employed to plan, organize, implement, delegate, control, and measure, I likewise beseech everyone to do their part to make things better. I have three words written on the whiteboard in my office: *attitude, gratitude, action*. These are three words that I try to remember in my work life and home life. They are words that guide me as a husband, father, manager, at home, at work, and in the community. They are also words that all people and all leaders (and, after all, we are all leaders) can live by.

It is our collective attitude that determines whether or not we have fun at work, or for that matter at home. So many of us fall into the trap of bemoaning how hard we have to work, how little we are appreciated, how we don't have enough of anything—money, power, supplies, equipment, staff, etc. However, it is our attitude that makes our work valuable, valued, memorable, a source of pride, and a positive contribution to the betterment of the workplace and society.

Our approach to work and our attitude toward life can make a huge difference. As a young man, I spent many hours fishing with my father. Often hours would go by without so much as a nibble or meaningful action of any kind. However, what was more meaningful to me were the chats we had about life, careers, and our contribution to society. One of his key messages was always that a person's vocation was not nearly as important as his approach, his enthusiasm, and his dedication to his chosen profession. He would say to me, "I don't give a damn what you choose to be, but if you choose to be a garbage man, just make sure you're the best garbage man who ever walked the face of the earth."

Perhaps Dr. Martin Luther King Jr. was a bit more eloquent when he said, "If a man is called to be a street sweeper, he should sweep streets even as Michelangelo painted or Beethoven composed music, or Shakespeare wrote poetry. He should sweep streets so well that all the hosts of heaven and earth will pause to say, 'Here lived a great street sweeper who did his job well.'" That is what attitude is all about. Whether you choose to be a stay-at-home mom, a company president, or the organizational receptionist, be the best you can possibly be.

We can complain about how nasty others are to us. We can claim that schedules aren't fair. We can protest that our work is no fun, that we get no respect, or dozens of other workplace concerns. However, responsibility always lies with each and every one of us and in our attitude toward life and work. Many writers have spoken about attitude when it comes to work, and have noted the importance of being passionate about your work. It's not just a job.

In addition to *attitude* is the need for a daily reflection on *gratitude*. We have so much to be thankful for, and yet so many of us don't appreciate the good things we have, always desiring more and better. We need to be thankful for our friends and families, who are so often there to share with us and support us. Most of us enjoy good health but lack the wisdom to truly appreciate its value. A wise man once told me, "I used to complain about my slippers until I met a man with no feet."

We have so much to be thankful for. We are all part of many different teams. Those teams may be our families, work teams, leadership teams, community teams, boards, unions, or parks associations. Frankly, if we do not appreciate every member of our team and fail to realize how important each and every member is, we become that much less effective. Andrew Carnegie said, "No man will make a great leader who wants to do it all himself or to get all the credit for doing it." We have so much to be thankful for.

Finally, I believe in *action*. There is an old adage that says the smallest of actions is better than the greatest of intentions. We can take steps to make our personal lives and our workplaces better, but we have to take action. Talk is cheap, as my father used to tell me. Fear is usually the cause of inaction: fear of failure, fear of success and how it may raise the bar for us, fear of criticism, fear of the unknown, fear of simply taking the first step in a journey of a thousand miles. But each one of us, no matter what our role, can make things happen.

In the movie *The Fellowship of the Ring* (the first film in the *Lord of the Rings* trilogy), there is a scene where Frodo Baggins tells the elf queen, Galadriel, that he no longer wants the role of being a ring bearer, as it is too much of burden and he is "only a hobbit." However, she explains to him simply that, "Even the smallest person could change the course of the future." I regularly encourage all leaders (and we are all leaders) to work diligently every day to make someone's life a little bit better. It seems simple enough, but it does require some effort.

As my good friend Dan Carter said in his book *Right Time Now*, "Remember the true gift of life is making an impact on someone else's life because we have been created at this time and at this moment to help ... There is no need to wait for someone else—it is the right time now. If we act together, we'll not only make our communities a better place, but we will truly find our assignment in life."(3) At the end of each day, we should take a few minutes to reflect on how we have helped to make someone's life a bit better, how we have made our organizations better, or how our sons and daughters have grown because of our efforts. That is true leadership.

Leadership Themes
In addition to gratitude, attitude, and action, other themes weave their way through every other aspect of leadership. Those themes are communication, relationships, discipline, and education.

Communication

I was once told by a former hospital CEO that the two most difficult jobs in any organization are HR and communications. He told me that HR is difficult only because so many people sincerely believe that they understand all there is to know about people. As for communications, everybody claims to know how to communicate. Obviously, he was being a tad facetious; he did not necessarily believe that these two jobs were literally the most difficult. However, effective communication was one of the key leadership principles that I promoted in *Common Sense Leadership*. In fact, the 7 Key Skills that I spoke of then are worth repeating now.

1. Listen carefully to what others tell you. The good Lord gave us two ears and one mouth so we could listen twice as much as we spoke.
2. Maintain an open-door policy. It conveys the impression that you are open to a free exchange of information and the sharing of new ideas.
3. Be approachable and available. Leaving the door open is no good if folks are afraid to enter.
4. Promote face-to-face communication. Make it comfortable. Don't rely on texting. Do coffee, breakfast, or lunch. The personal touch is worth a fortune.
5. Remember the importance of nonverbal aspects of communication. Does your body language tell others things that your words do not?
6. Always be candid in your communication. Leave politics to politicians. No need to be brutally frank—just open and honest.
7. Be consistent, not up one day and down the next. Remain calm under fire and remember, the stars only come out at night. People need you when things are darkest. Anybody can lead when things are going well.

Effective communication cuts through every aspect of leadership covered by this book. It contributes positively to our culture, allows us to have fun, shows respect, resolves conflict, and so on. Don't ever underestimate the power and importance of good communication skills.

Relationships

We achieve very little in life by ourselves. There are other members of our teams, those whom we lead, people we work with, customers to consider, and myriad other stakeholders who make our world go 'round. I can think of no better way to be successful at any level of any organization, in the community or at home, than to build a network of positive, effective relationships. The more people we know, the more networking we do. Assuming they are the right kind of people (as opposed to the kind you find in police lineups), the more help we both ask for and offer, the more likely it is that we will all benefit. Remember, a person's wealth is not measured in material possessions but rather by the number of friends and associates whose company he enjoys.

Discipline

The discipline that I refer to here is not the heavy-handed type so often discussed in employee relations or labour relations situations (e.g., warning, suspension, termination). Rather, it is self-discipline so often expected of us in life. It doesn't matter if we need to exercise more, lose weight, stop smoking, go to church, be pleasant with others, or simply instill new leadership habits. All these require discipline. It is my understanding that it takes 21 days to establish a new habit or to break an old one. There are plenty of tips in the following pages to develop meaningful and productive new habits, some of which will require time and energy. Remember that leadership is not easy. It takes hard work, day in and day out. We can't simply decide to make a change one day and that will be it forever more. It takes at least 21 days. But the effort will always be worthwhile, and there is no time like the present to get started. I have already referenced Dan Carter, and I will now add a comment by Mother Teresa, who said, "Yesterday is gone. Tomorrow has not yet come. We have only today. Let us begin."

Education

Finally, regardless of everything we do as leaders, we have an obligation to be educators. We inspire and improve those around us by developing them and by teaching them the lessons of life and of the workplace. Our role is to make them better, whether they are our children, our staff, our colleagues, or our community. As it was once pointed out to me, the only member of the orchestra who doesn't make a sound is the conductor. It is his job, as leader, to make everybody else sound better. Leadership is not complicated. However, it is hard work, and fortunately it is practised by so many people in so many ways and by so many for no obvious monetary reward whatsoever. So, for all the mothers, parents, grandparents, executives, managers, community leaders, and others, let us all join together to make changes that ultimately create a better home life, a better community and a better work world for everyone. I hope the following pages reflect a new attitude at work. Things need to move away from command and control and become more flexible, more accommodating, and more fun. I want all the managers and leaders out there to start truly enjoying their work. It's okay to have fun at work. It certainly makes it less stressful. But we need to start somewhere, so as Mother Teresa said, "Let us begin."

Key Messages

- We are all leaders, regardless of our title.
- Attitude determines whether we enjoy our work.
- We should all make more time for gratitude.
- We can all take action, no matter how small, to make our workplace better.
- Communication, relationship building, discipline, and education are strengths of effective leaders.

Chapter 2:

Leading by Serving

A sales rep, an administration clerk, and their manager were walking to lunch one day when they found an antique oil lamp. They rubbed the lamp and a genie emerged from it. The genie said to them, "Because you have rescued me, I am now prepared to grant each of you one wish."

"Me first, me first," shouted the admin clerk. "I want to be in the Bahamas, driving a speedboat, without a care in the world." With a puff she was gone.

"Me next, me next," the sales rep said. "I want to be in Hawaii, relaxing on the beach with my personal masseuse, an endless supply of piña coladas, and the love of my life." In a flash, he was also gone.

"Okay, you're next," said the genie to the manager.

The manager hesitated only for a moment and then said, "I want those two back in the office as soon as their lunch hour is finished."

The moral to this story: always let your boss have the first say. However, that is not necessarily the first rule of leading by serving others, because in that capacity, managers, as leaders, are more inclined to address the needs of their staff to ensure that they grow as people.

I am always reluctant to place labels on anything that is related to leadership practices or principles. I have seen too many instances where organizational leaders attend a conference and hear about the latest leadership movements. They return to the workplace intent on implementing the new approach to business without a full consideration of whether or not it makes sense or is practical for their purposes. As a result, I am not here to convince anybody that they should now identify with servant leadership as a be-all and end-all.

In reality, I do not consider servant leadership to be a model of any kind. Rather, it is more of an operating mantra, a philosophy, or a way of behaving. It is not a set of skills that we use in the same way that management is a series of roles that we perform. It is a way of being and a way of conducting ourselves in the workplace. It is an approach that results in the workplace being far more enjoyable for staff than it might otherwise be. Practise these principles and both you and your staff might just enjoy your work.

My good friend Dr. Hugh Drouin has this to say about the nature of servant leadership:

> Servant leadership is a "way of being" that requires that we integrate the principles of servant leadership into our daily leadership practices. The "way of being" deals with the condition of our interior life which impacts the outward expression of positive, affirming leadership behaviours. The challenge is to keep our internal life growing so we can live out the servant leadership principles for the benefit of others whom we come into contact with in our daily interactions. As such, servant leadership is not a set of techniques but a way of living our life and practice.

Three things flow, in turn, from Hugh's description that demand further examination. First, what is meant by the "way of being" and what he refers to as our "internal life"? Second, what is the exact nature of servant leadership behaviour? What does it look like? Third, what are the principles of servant leadership? Let's turn our attention to these three issues.

1. Way of being

The way of being is the way that we connect with other human beings. As James A. Autry puts it, "'How does your spirituality find expression in the workplace, in your attitude about your work, in your relationships with your employees, peers, colleagues, customers, vendors, and others?' That's the question and the challenge, because it is in your attitude and behaviour as well as your relationships that your spirituality expresses itself at work—an expression that is most often manifest as service."(4) Further, he proposes that there are five ways of being that are critical for all of us to have those relationships thrive: being authentic, being vulnerable, being accepting, being present, and being useful.

Being *authentic* simply means being reliable and consistent so that those who you deal with daily know what to expect from you. It's not a matter of waiting to see which side of the bed you got up on or what behaviour, action, or attitude is called for in a given situation. Rather, it involves having people trust that what you say is also how you conduct yourself. In *Common Sense Leadership* I talked about the importance that staff place on organization leaders "walking the talk." As Lance Secretan says, "Authenticity is the alignment of head, mouth, heart, and feet—thinking, saying, feeling, and doing the same thing—consistently. This builds trust, and followers love leaders they can trust."(5)

Being *vulnerable* is nothing more than being in touch with your own feelings and having the capacity to share those feelings with those around you. It is being sensitive to the needs of others and being able to say, "I screwed up." None of us is perfect, but we can all relate to leaders who sincerely acknowledge their mistakes and ask the forgiveness of others. The sincerity attached to these actions is important, as we all know people who have said "sorry" and didn't mean it. That sort of conduct takes relationships to an entirely different level, a lower one. However, if we look back to the Tylenol scare that Johnson & Johnson faced back in the 1980s, their leadership stepped up to the plate and said, "We made a mistake, and now we plan to make things better." They walked the talk. Their operating principles aligned with their behaviour. It was the right thing to do. People can follow that conduct.

Sometimes, we must accept the faults, failures, and weaknesses of others. We do so without judgment because they are part of our team, family, or community. We need to trust others. This does not mean that we do not subject their actions and behaviours to occasional critical assessment. This is not blind faith but rather acceptance that there may well be differences of opinion or disagreements when any people come together for any common purpose. We promote honesty, transparency, and openness. That is the nature of a "team." We have their back, and they have ours.

We also conduct ourselves in the *present*. We can forget about what happened 10 years ago. That is history, and it is now time to move on. Even though I suggest that leaders continuously scan the horizon and be ready for change when it happens, we must, nonetheless, stay focused on what is before us. We are engaged in our roles as managers and as leaders and with what is happening right now.

Finally, we must still *be useful*. Servant leadership is nice as an operating philosophy, but it must also be practical. I indicated earlier that one key role of leaders is to make the people around them better. We do this by coaching, counseling, cheerleading, and educating. We do it by serving as a resource for our staff. We help them with their conflicts. We understand that they are fighting battles at work and at home, and through that understanding we are occasionally able to help them to improve their lives and their utility at the workplace. In fact, by serving our team, we make them better, and that is how we become better leaders.

2. Servant leadership principles

Servant leadership is a way of being with each other in the workplace. Our role as leader is to serve others and the ultimate goal is that those we serve grow as persons. They become better, and if everybody we serve in turn becomes better as employees and as persons, there are immense benefits, not only for the workplace but also for the community as a whole. How do they become better? We measure our success by our ability to respond positively to questions such as the following:

- Are they healthier?
- Are they wiser?
- Are they freer or more autonomous?
- Are they more inclined, following their interactions with us to become servant leaders themselves, or are they at least willing to accept their role to serve others for the overall betterment of the team or the community?
- Most importantly, do the least privileged of society benefit, or are they at least not further deprived? While not every action we take will have an immediate and obvious impact on the least privileged, we need to keep their welfare foremost in our minds and in our actions.

In short, servant leadership means:

- Caring for others
- Being present for others when they need us most
- Not holding on to our egos but rather being authentic
- Creating the right place, atmosphere, and culture where policy and behaviour are consistent with one another

- Paying attention to people and being sensitive to their needs
- Building an attitude that is centred on forgiving and forgetting
- Being concerned about quality relationships
- Being responsible for followers, for the empowerment of self and others, for society, and for those who are disadvantaged
- Getting followers to also be prepared to sacrifice for the good of the whole

3. Ten principles of servant leadership

There are 10 principle behaviours most closely associated with servant leadership.

1. Listening
2. Empathy
3. Healing
4. Awareness
5. Persuasion
6. Conceptualization
7. Foresight
8. Stewardship
9. Commitment to the growth of people
10. Building community

Each of these deserves a brief description.

1. **Listening.** When I speak of "listening," I don't mean simply hearing what somebody is saying but rather engaging in real concentration and caring about what the other party is saying to you. There is an old saying: "Seek to understand, not to be understood." As my parents told me, "The good Lord gave you two ears and one mouth so you can listen twice as much as what you speak!" We speak at the rate of 125–250 words per minute, but the human brain has the capacity to think at something like 1,000–3,000 words per minute. Sadly, that may mean that we

have a lot of spare time to think when someone is speaking to us. Instead of thinking about other matters, managers and leaders need to practise listening very carefully to what staff, colleagues, bosses, customers, suppliers, and other stakeholders are saying. Too often, we engage in multitasking, anticipating what others are about to say instead of waiting for them to say it or we are simply not focused on the message being delivered. I have also spoken about maintaining an open-door policy, but to do so one must be available and approachable. If your door is open but you aren't there or people feel you are unapproachable, good communications will be stifled. Also, remember your body language. Certain actions convey certain sentiments. If you look people in the eye when they are speaking to you and generally lean into the conversation, it conveys a belief on their part that you are genuinely listening to what they are saying. Listening intently to others is good for their self-esteem and is more likely to convince them that you respect them and value them. However, active listening takes time and practice and requires inner peace. The practice can come from quiet reflection, meditation, or other means intended to quiet our mind. We need to listen with more focus and attention. If we do, then we demonstrate the true meaning of servant leadership in our daily workplace interactions.

2. **Empathy.** Empathy is the capacity to feel a connection with the feelings and ideas of others. Every employee who works with you, in your department or elsewhere in the organization, has gifts they bring to the job. Those gifts include their education, experience, knowledge, talents, abilities, and network of contacts. For each one of us, these gifts are unique and make us what we truly are as individuals. A servant leader will accept every person as an individual and will respect his or her unique gifts. By doing this, we can identify with an entire spectrum of individuals because they not only bring their unique nature to

the job, but they also bring their faults, trials, and tribulations. We all face, at one time or another, health concerns, financial issues or other personal or professional challenges. When we empathize with the feelings of others, we can understand their hurt and are prepared to put ourselves in their place. Even when co-workers let us down, we must accept what is good about them while rejecting the behaviour or performance that let us down. Empathy allows us to feel sadness when our staff or colleagues feel sadness and to celebrate when they feel exuberant. It is all part of being human, and although it is not always easy, we can develop these skills. We'll consider this further in chapter 3, "Leading with Emotional Intelligence."

3. **Healing.** Healing occurs when an individual or some group of people have suffered some hurt or harm. It is true second nature for the servant leader to take on the responsibility of trying to make that hurt better. It starts with striving to heal ourselves at difficult times and continues when our staff need the same healing. The search for wholeness actually reflects our desire to be more complete as human beings. Most of us strive to achieve a position in our lives where we truly matter to something or for someone. A state of wholeness is achieved when we are physically, emotionally, socially, and spiritually sound in both our professional and personal lives. Compassion, like empathy, is the capacity to understand the plight of others, feel for them, and offer support, as a leader and as an organization, to help them through their difficult times. Above all else, we have an obligation to offer our staff and colleagues hope by seeing their goodness, being optimistic, regarding problems as opportunities and forging ahead when others may quit. Remember that we have the best chance to serve others when the world is at its darkest.

4. **Awareness**. Both self-awareness and a general awareness of the needs of our staff makes the servant leader stronger and

an even greater resource for the organization. We must always be aware of what is happening around us and encourage our staff to be equally aware. This is the essence of a learning organization. Remembering that my own definition of a leader is one who inspires others to achieve greater personal heights or higher levels of performance, a servant leader will provide support and assistance to staff to help them grow and develop in their current role as well as prepare them for future roles. As Graham Lowe points out,

> Vibrant workplaces also encourage individual and group learning. Active learning is therefore a mark of the inspired employee. Leading thinkers on learning organizations agree that people learn in workplaces through a process that extends over time, is collaborative, and is based on continual knowledge acquisition and dissemination. Learning helps workers to avoid repeating mistakes, to reproduce successes, and to discover new work methods, services or products.(6)

Awareness leads to greater learning, which in turn leads to a more inspirational workplace.

5. **Persuasion.** Servant leaders must use persuasion in their relations with their staff. As a result, they never resort to positional power to impose their will. Persuasion is always respectful and gentle. As Gandhi observed, "In a gentle way, you can shake the world." The story is told of two competing sheep farmers, one of whom walked in front of his sheep herd, leading the way. The sheep followed at their leisure, feeling free and easy. The quality of the mutton and wool from this herd was outstanding. The other farmer walked behind the flock, driving them along with his staff. These sheep were stressed by the constant prodding, and the quality of their mutton and wool

was poor. The same is true of organizational leadership. Drive your staff and the result will invariably be a lack of enthusiasm, energy, and support from them for your initiatives. Lead them, using encouragement and gentle persuasion, and the result is more likely to be a positive attitude, a sense of empowerment, and undying support for your leadership.

6. **Conceptualization.** Servant leaders think beyond day-to-day realities. To use an overworked phrase, they "think outside the box." We need to dream great dreams. As Robert Kennedy once said, "There are those who look at things the way they are, and ask why ... I dream of things that never were and ask why not?" Stephen R. Covey, in *The 7 Habits of Highly Effective People*, speaks of the need to begin with the end in mind. When we plan to take a trip, we know our starting point and we know our final destination. That is like beginning with the end in mind. Others speak of the practice of developing big, hairy, audacious goals (BHAGs). Either way, as leaders, we need to stretch our current realities. What do we see in the future for ourselves and our departments? Determining what the future holds is the leader's role, and it requires some foresight, some good guesses, and an understanding of your work environment.

7. **Foresight.** Foresight is the ability to use the skill of conceptualization to plan for the future. As the Cheshire cat in *Alice in Wonderland* said, "If you don't know where you are going, any road will get you there." Servant leaders not only dream the great dreams, but they also have the ability to draw up the roadmap that will take them from point A to point B. However, this is not a single-minded determination to chart the course for the future of the department or the organization. Again, it is using the other principles of servant leadership, listening to the viewpoints of others, engaging their input, and using the gifts that everyone has to offer, gaining

consensus to determining the way forward. Servant leaders anticipate roadblocks and go around, over, or through them. They perpetually scan the horizon and see new possibilities where others often see none. Servant leaders do not dwell on the past but learn from it to discover a better future.

8. **Stewardship**. This is the responsibility imposed upon each of us (but for the purposes of this discussion, mainly managers and leaders) to manage the part of the organization that has been entrusted to us. We are expected to manage in such a way that our organization benefits from our efforts and is therefore more successful. Further, the way we manage should not only result in success, but it must be done in ways considered to be right, just, fair and resulting in minimal harm to others. Stewardship also means looking to build something for the future, making a meaningful contribution to the community for generations to come. There is an element of corporate social responsibility to all this. We should all include, within our scope of responsibilities, stewardship for the community, for our environment, and for the promotion of principles of equality and diversity.

9. **Commitment to the growth of people.** As someone with a strong background in HR, I believe this principle is of critical importance. The staff of our organizations cannot be considered as just "human resources." While it is true that they have their roles to perform with their job descriptions and routines, they also, individually and collectively, offer us so much more. Servant leaders must be deeply committed to the personal, professional, and spiritual growth of all staff. Remember that one of our leadership roles is to make those around us better. As I noted previously, the role of any leader is to inspire and make those around him or her better. Sadly, in difficult financial times, all too often the first victims of a "hack and burn" mentality are staff education, training, and development. As a result,

organizations that look to balance the books on the backs of these relatively minor accounts are being penny wise and pound foolish. On balance, this is simply shortsighted. We must always promote the development of staff, nurturing a culture of creativity, risk-taking, and innovation. With every new idea, with every new learning, staff increase their capacity to contribute. As Oliver Wendell Holmes noted, "Man's mind, once stretched by a new idea, never regains its original dimensions."

10. **Building Community.** The Industrial Revolution brought a new concept of "workplace" with it. In many instances the workplace became a manufacturing environment, where efficiency meant having each employee performing relatively few tasks but doing them extremely well as part of an assembly or production line. Notwithstanding that efficiency, too many people remain dissatisfied with a workplace where their individual talents and contributions remain isolated and limited in scope. As a result, there has increasingly been a movement to create a sense of community in the workplace. We speak of the importance of *workplace values* or wanting to be an *employer of choice*. Many of us will recall the Dofasco motto of the 1970s, which proclaimed, "Our product is steel. Our strength is people." Organizational leadership and a true servant leader should be committed to creating a workplace that enjoys a sense of community, where the needs of the staff come before the needs of the leader. When that sense of community is present, all staff enjoy greater peace, stability, and commitment to work. We enjoy the company of each other and the very positive work relationships that come with that culture.

What is intriguing about the principles and values espoused by servant leadership is that they support a manner of behaviour that I have preached for many years.

Servant Leadership Seems like a No-Brainer. Why Fight It?

Let's be honest. Some will always resist any initiative for any reason whatsoever. Justifications include "It wasn't my idea in the first place," "It's not the way I do things," and "I know what I'm doing. Who are you to tell me how to do my job?" However, outside these non-reasons, there are several barriers to full implementation of servant leadership in any organization:

- **"It's just another fad."** Robert Greenleaf first coined the term *servant leadership* in 1970. After 42 years, it can hardly be considered another fad.
- **"I'm too busy fighting fires."** Remember that servant leadership is actually a way of behaving. Behaviour is encouraged that leads to the prevention of fires in the organization. Invest your time and energy in the proper leadership principles and the result will be fewer fires to fight.
- **"The boss just isn't into it."** Who cares? As Robin Sharma, author of *The Leader Who Had No Title*, notes, "You need to be the CEO of your own job." The fact that your boss doesn't practise servant leadership is no reason to guide your behaviour down the wrong path. The success that you enjoy by practising servant leadership may encourage others, including the boss, to do likewise. Developing people is not limited to developing only those that report to you. A true leader develops everyone around him or her.
- **"If it ain't broke, don't fix it."** If I can heat my home for $1,000 a year but, through improved conservation practices, I can reduce my costs to $800 a year, wouldn't I want to consider the new approach? Of course. There is always room to improve. As the saying goes, "You don't have to be sick to get better."
- **"I don't like the idea of giving up our management rights."** Under servant leadership, you are still responsible for managing your department or service. As a manager, you engage in

various roles. However, practising servant leadership allows you to be far more effective as a manager. Don't worry. The inmates aren't running the prison under servant leadership.

In summary, I encourage every manager and leader to practise the principles behind servant leadership. Even if you don't label it as such, it will be well worth any effort you put into it.

Key Messages
Servant Leadership—How Can I Help You?

When we were kids, we were taught the importance of fairness, of being kind to others, and of never intentionally harming another person or animal. Don't lose sight of the value of these lessons.

- Authenticity is the alignment of the head, mouth, heart, and feet with our thoughts, words, feelings, and actions.
- Become an active listener. Remember: you have two ears and one mouth.
- Be committed to growth in yourself and others. Never allow yourself to believe that you have no more to learn. Learning should happen every day of your life, and part of your role as a leader is to educate others.

Chapter 3:

Leading with Emotional Intelligence

How many times have you heard somebody exclaim something akin to, "Bob is incredibly bright. In fact, he has a genius-level IQ"? That sort of exclamation is followed by the usual oohs and ahhhs, with the assembled audience seemingly duly impressed. However, many of these geniuses seem unable simply to get along with other people. In some cases, we are told they have the personality of a slug, or it's part of their makeup that they don't get along with others. Sometimes they've been like that since they were kids. We're all familiar with this type of individual.

On the other hand, there are those who do not possess the same IQ but do extremely well in life because they get along with others or because they manage social situations so well. For these individuals, the key to success is their high level of emotional intelligence.

Emotional intelligence is a term that many managers/leaders have heard but don't fully appreciate what it means to them on a daily basis. A better understanding of the concept of emotional intelligence may help them improve their leadership performance, improving the quality of life in the workplace.

Emotional Intelligence Defined

To clarify, while they refer to two different things, the terms *emotional intelligence* (EI) and *emotional quotient* (EQ) are often used interchangeably. EI is the ability to understand ourselves and others, while EQ is the measure of that ability. Steven Stein and Howard Book have defined emotional intelligence in *The EQ Edge* as

> "a set of skills that enables us to make our way in a complex world—the personal, social and survival aspects of overall intelligence, the elusive common sense and sensitivity that are essential to effective daily functioning. In everyday language, emotional intelligence is what we commonly refer to as 'street smarts,' or that uncommon ability we label 'common sense.' It has to do with the ability to read the political and social environment, and landscape them; to intuitively grasp what others want and need, what their strengths and weaknesses are; to remain unruffled by stress; and to be engaging, the kind of person that others want to be around."(7)

Bradberry and Greaves defined it as "the ability to recognize and understand emotions in yourself and others, and your ability to use this awareness to manage your behaviour and relationships."(8)

Emotional intelligence, like servant leadership, is not a fad or trend. We have been talking about it for more than 30 years, and while it sometimes appears to be something intended for classes in organizational psychology or sociology of work, nothing could be further from the truth.

The roles we perform as managers are separate from our performance as leaders. As managers, we must plan, organize, implement, delegate, control, measure, and make decisions. Leadership involves how we make these things happen, and one of the most important parts of leadership is the development of the so-called soft skills. Although the exact nature of these soft skills may differ from one expert to the next, for the purposes of this discussion, they include the following skills: being aware of ourselves, being able to manage ourselves, being aware of the social world in which we function, and being able to manage our social relationships.

As noted, no matter how bright we are, if we lack the capacity to consider the feelings of others, to read social situations, or to understand how people behave, then we have a low level of emotional intelligence. This in turn adversely affects our ability to lead others.

There are some components of servant leadership (empathy, for example) that are also considered to be part of our emotional intelligence. Once again, I am loathe to label things any more than necessary, but an understanding of the skill sets associated with emotional intelligence is in order.

I recall interviewing organizational leaders for *Common Sense Leadership* to understand what it took to be more than just a manager for staff. I wanted to understand what it takes to be a great leader. I remember being intrigued by the common words they used to describe their activities, as well as how their own staff described them as leaders. I didn't recognize these qualities as part of emotional intelligence at that time. They mentioned the following:

- Being approachable
- Being a mentor to their staff
- Being visionary
- Being a good communicator
- Being a helmsman
- Having passion for their work
- Being captain of the team
- Being decisive
- Showing consistency

- Promoting learning and development of self and staff
- Celebrating success
- Having integrity
- Remaining calm at all times
- Demonstrating good common sense
- Remaining humble
- Being open to new initiatives
- Empowering staff
- Leading by example

As it turns out, all these are features of emotional intelligence. No wonder people wanted to come work for these leaders, and once there, staff were reluctant to leave.

So, how do we begin to use this information effectively? How do we improve upon our own emotional intelligence? First, let us remember that the CEO should set the standard for the organization. He or she will attract other leaders of like mind, spirit, and attitude. They in turn should attract directors, managers, and supervisors who are similar in nature.

This domino effect should serve the entire organization well. The problem arises when the CEO is a miserable SOB or if poor hiring decisions are made and other members of the organization are engaged who have the wrong type of personality or the wrong level of emotional intelligence. To be honest, it can all start with a CEO who is simply nice to others and smiles a lot. I know this doesn't sound very profound, but any of us can answer a very simple question: Would I rather work for someone who is nice and who is consistent or someone who is a grouch? Few of us would pick the latter.

If you, as a leader, come to work in good humour, smiling at everybody you meet and enjoying a positive, upbeat attitude, the work environment will reflect a similar degree of positivism. In addition to a personal and individual attitude, which needs to be positive, remember that part of emotional intelligence includes the ability to get along with others. This will include your own team and staff, colleagues, and members of the senior leadership team for those at that level of the organization. When people get along, the workplace is more fun to be part of. Speaking from experience, I can assure you that senior teams that don't get along drain your enthusiasm for the job, and that negativism ultimately pervades the entire organization.

There are many ways to measure and define emotional intelligence. It can be fairly stated that no one person can be great in all aspects of emotional intelligence. In fact, circumstances may dictate which EI strategies may best be used at any given point in time. Much like the selection of clubs in my golf bag, circumstances dictate which one I use at any given time. Unfortunately, the deficiencies in my golf game are not limited to club selection.

For all of us, it is critical that we understand and come to grips with our inner self and our ability to manage our emotions and our reactions to situations. This self-understanding and self-management, when combined with our understanding of why people behave as they do and how we can manage our relations with others, determines the quality of our emotional intelligence. Exit interviews have shown me over the years that staff leave organizations because of poor management, not pay and benefits. The compensation plan and the employer's reputation may attract staff, but in reality, people join companies while they leave bad managers.

Emotional intelligence is the most important aspect of a manager's job, but when we are hiring a manager, too often we look first for a diploma or years of experience and are seemingly less concerned about other, equally critical, aspects of the hire. As Bradberry and Greaves note, "We enter the workforce knowing how to read, write, and report on bodies of knowledge, but too often, we lack the skills to manage our emotions in the heat of the challenging problems that we face. Good decisions require far more than factual knowledge. They are made using self-knowledge and emotional mastery when they're needed most."(9)

Our emotions require a degree of mastery. We will react to situations in ways that are often quite uncontrollable. However, we must learn to control the thoughts that follow those situations. So, what is it that we, as managers and leaders, must learn to do better? The following is a brief summary of three models or approaches to emotional intelligence that may help us understand the topic. Following these summaries, I have added my own interpretation of emotional intelligence. As with most models on any subject, there are similarities just as there are differences. Personally, I do not claim to follow or support any one model in its entirety, but that is primarily because I don't tend to label my behaviours as such. It is important that we recognize the overall themes and work hard to develop and learn how to apply emotional intelligence skills for ourselves and others.

Steven J. Stein and Howard E. Book, *The EQ Edge*

Stein and Book, while appreciating the value of IQ as a measure of intelligence, promote a greater emphasis on emotional intelligence as a better measure in so many ways. They contend that many organizational problems are unrelated to fields such as accounting or strategic planning but are rather the result of poor communications and a failure to understand one another. Put another way, you may have an exceptionally high IQ, but if you perpetually turn people off with a bad attitude, arrogance, or a simple lack of personal sensitivity, you will not enjoy the same success that you may otherwise enjoy. In their minds, EI represents the personal, social, and survival aspects of our total being. Common sense, intuition, and sensitivity to the needs of others, along with an innate appreciation of organizational politics, are key competencies for any manager/leader. They also speak to the need to remain calm in any circumstances. Their model includes the following elements:

- **Intrapersonal.** This relates to an understanding of the "inner self," a concept referred to in servant leadership as well. If you are in touch with and feel good about yourself, you "are able to express your feelings, live and work independently, feel strong, and have confidence in expressing your ideas and beliefs." Everybody has feelings. That is simple human nature. However, the ability to express those feelings in a positive fashion is a large part of who we are. Generally, it is also important for each of us to be happy in our own skin, and while each of us should constantly strive to be better, those with strong intrapersonal skills recognize that they have both strengths and weaknesses and accept that fact without taking on undue stress.
- **Interpersonal.** This element relates to one's ability to interact well with others in a variety of situations. If you have good interpersonal skills, you generally will function well as a member of the team and you will be able to empathize with others. It also involves our obligation to our family and the community at large to be a productive member of society and give back to it for the benefit of others. In general, those with a high level of emotional intelligence get along well with others.
- **Adaptability.** Life is not always easy, nor is it predictable. As managers and leaders, we are put to the test every day as new and challenging situations confront us. Adaptable managers respond effectively to these challenges. This realm includes our ability to adjust to our daily reality, no matter what comes our way. It also looks at the ability of individuals to be flexible and problem solve on the fly.
- **Stress management.** We all need help sometimes to deal with life's problems and challenges without losing control. In the discussion about work/life balance, it is noted that, in today's world, all of us are often tested by life's daily challenges. This model discusses our ability to adjust to adversity in our personal or professional lives plus our capacity to manage stress without "blowing a gasket." We all have days where

keeping everything under control is a supreme challenge. Those with a high degree of emotional intelligence are able to keep everything appropriately together and stay calm.

- **General mood.** All of us have the opportunity to view our work and our lives generally as the glass being half full or half empty. We can approach things with a positive outlook with a high degree of happiness and contentment or we can be more negative and pessimistic in our views. Our general mood will reflect how satisfied we are with ourselves, others, and life in general and essentially asks of individuals if they see their glass as half empty or half full.

Travis Bradberry and Jean Greaves, *Emotional Intelligence 2.0*

The approach taken by Bradberry and Greaves is slightly different from that of Stein and Book in that they break EI into four broad groupings or strategies.

- **Self-awareness.** Emotions are what make us human beings. For each of us, some emotions are stronger than others, and at the same time they vary in intensity from one person to the next. Self-awareness is not only the ability to recognize your own emotions and the intensity of each but also to understand the nature of people, events and issues that cause you to react as you do. There are situations in life that cause us to laugh or cry or to get angry. One of the lessons that I was told as a young boy was that "real men don't cry." All the men in the crowd can debate whether or not this is true, or whether it is even a good lesson. The truth is that it really doesn't matter much. There are things that may make me cry, just as they do for everybody else. Part of self-awareness is working to understand what leads me to react in that way. Again, we all have feelings, and part of emotional intelligence is acknowledging and understanding those feelings and understanding the triggers that cause us to act or react to certain situations.

- **Self-Management.** Self-management is the ability to control our emotions in order to achieve the most positive outcomes possible. If you enjoy a high degree of self-management, you set meaningful goals for yourself and adhere to them as much as possible. You know how to control emotions and know that "things will always seem better in the morning." You know what circumstances trigger what reactions for yourself and regardless of those triggers and reactions, you are able to keep things in perspective. By observing others and by using parents, leaders, coaches, and mentors, you try to learn something about yourself that helps make you better each and every day. In the next chapter, I deal with the issue of work/life balance, which is precisely what self-management is all about—maintaining stability and ensuring you take time for personal renewal. This may include daily downtime, rest times during the week (including getting enough sleep), and the enjoyment of an annual vacation.

- **Social awareness.** Once we have mastered ourselves and our own emotions, we must ensure that we understand the nature of our relations with others, can pick up on their emotions, can perceive what others are thinking and feeling, and are sensitive to their needs. Listening and observing are key skills. Truly communicating with others will help in this regard. This means not only listening to the words others are sharing with us but also observing and acknowledging their emotions, their body language, and other clues to the true message. We can improve our social awareness by remembering people's names and truly understanding them as individuals. We need to recognize that everybody has different personal space needs, and we all have issues that we are facing. Be sensitive to such factors. An excellent vehicle to help improve social awareness is what many training sessions have dubbed as "walk a day in my shoes," a program used most often in social service–type organizations. It helps staff to better understand client needs, hopefully leading to better delivery of services.

- **Relationship management.** Once we are aware of social relationships and the moods and feelings of others, it is time to manage those relationships. These are the bonds that develop over time, and they are refined with clear communication, solid conflict resolution, and simply being kind, decent, and sensitive to the needs of others. It also helps to have a common history, as well as common likes and dislikes, but this is not critical. Personal relationships, especially those we create when we live together with someone else, are often tenuous, but work relationships are prone to an equal degree of stress and emotion. We can improve our relationship management by improving our communication skills, promoting active listening, and being sensitive to the needs and feelings of others. As a manager, you can to promote and maintain an open-door policy, and when you make decisions, be consistent with your approach, stay true to your values, and be prepared to explain them so staff understand them. Taking the old parental approach of "just because" or "Daddy knows best" is not only not productive, it can be downright harmful. Trust others and work hard to make sure they trust you. Be kind, courteous, and nice to others. Show them you care.

Daniel Goleman, Richard Boyatzis, and Annie McKee, *Primal Leadership*

The approach Goleman et al. use is similar to that taken by Bradberry and Greaves in that they break the topic of emotional intelligence into the same four "domains," as they call them, with a multitude of competencies within each domain. The four domains differ from those used by Bradberry and Greaves in that they refer to competencies. However, very strong similarities may still be noted.

- **Self-awareness competencies.** This is our ability to read and understand our own feelings, emotions, and sensitivities and to recognize the impact they have on others. It is also important that we know our strengths and how to use them with confidence while, at the same time, learning to manage with our acknowledged weaknesses.

- **Self-management competencies.** Knowing the nature of our "self" is one thing, but being able to manage it is something totally different. These competencies enable us to use positive emotions to full advantage and keeping negative or disruptive emotions in check. Are we transparent, open, honest, and trustworthy? How do we deliver on those qualities? We must be able to adapt to changing circumstances and to have the initiative to seize upon opportunities when they are presented. As noted earlier, self-management also relates to our attitude and degree of optimism about life in general. Do we have the tendency to see the glass as half full, or is it half empty?

- **Social awareness competencies.** As with other models, this one involves the degree of empathy we show and the sensitivity demonstrated to the issues faced by others. We must be aware of the nature of our organization, its politics, history, culture, and even the industry or greater community that it is part of. Like servant leadership, social awareness competencies involve the degree of service shown toward staff, customers, family, and the community at large.

- **Relationship management competencies.** Having an understanding of our social world is one thing, but that knowledge must be combined with an ability to manage those relationships effectively. The competencies in this domain demonstrate our ability to not only inspire others but also to develop them as individuals and as staff. If we enjoy strong relationship management skills, we are adept at managing change and conflict, and most importantly we maintain a web of relationships while promoting teamwork and collaboration with a host of others.

Conclusions and Summary of Learnings

From my perspective, I like the breakdown in the final two models. These are simple but meaningful. In fact, if I refer back to the elements of leadership that I discussed in chapter 1, several become evident in this discussion of emotional intelligence. I mentioned the importance of good communications, relationship building, our leadership role in developing others, and the critical role played by our attitude. Therefore, I stress the following aspects of emotional intelligence for any organizational leader or manager:

- *Self-awareness* is the ability to know ourselves and have a good, comfortable grasp of our feelings. It's okay to feel either sadness or joy, and it is equally acceptable to let others know when you feel the way you do. That happens to people. You have to be happy in your own skin and quit worrying about being more like others—like movie stars or models. We all have strengths and weaknesses. Know yours and what they may mean for you, especially as it relates to your potential to grow and develop into the kind of person you want to be and that the world needs. Always keep a good perspective on life, and always maintain noble values.

- *Self-management* relates to our ability not only to understand ourselves but to do something with that understanding. Set goals for yourself and pursue them, always striving to be better. Your interest should not flow from a lack of happiness about who you are but rather from a desire to learn something every day, to be better and to strive to make the world a better place because of your contributions. You need to be at peace with your emotions, but you must not let them get the better of you. Part of self-management includes maintaining a sound work/life balance, and part of that is the ability to enjoy personal renewal through good eating habits, sufficient rest and vacation time, regular exercise, plus the enjoyment of continuous education and development.

- **Social awareness** includes our ability to get along well with others. It refers to our degree of empathy and respect for individuals but also, because organizations are complex social structures, we need to be aware of and sensitive to those aspects of organizational life. We need to appreciate that everyone has personal issues and needs their space. They also have emotions, strengths, and weaknesses that we need to be aware of. Understand organizational politics and culture as well as the roles that people must play in the organization.

- **Relationship management** is, as I have noted, a key feature of leadership for any of us. Because relationships are so important, a high degree of emotional intelligence will result in stronger, more effective communications with others. It will also enhance aspects of teamwork and promote the development and success of others. We have to manage change and conflict effectively because they too connect so closely to relationship management. Remember to be nice to others, to have fun, and to practise the Golden Rule. Keep your door always open and appreciate the good things that everyone brings to this world.

Many of us have had it drilled into our heads that as managers and leaders, we must be tough, like George S. Patton or Donald Trump in *The Apprentice*. While emotional intelligence does not take away any responsibility for making tough decisions, it does encourage us to consider the softer side of people management. It reminds us that we all have feelings and that we should see staff as more than simply "human resources." The sooner managers recognize that fact, the sooner they can get on with the all-important job of leading those people.

We all need to practise good emotional intelligence, and that involves understanding ourselves, managing our own emotions, understanding the nature of other people and their emotions, and managing our relationships with others. Our wealth is not measured by our material possessions but rather by the number of friends and associates we have and the quality of those relationships. EI can be learned and developed. We're never too old to change. Learn from yourself, from your experiences and mistakes, and learn from the experiences and mistakes of others.

Key Messages
Emotional Intelligence

Part of growing up for all of us is getting to know ourselves, getting to know others, and building relationships, a skill that is a key part of good leadership.

1. Understand the nature of yourself, your emotions, your feelings, and the triggers that cause you to behave as you do.
2. Learn to manage yourself and your emotions in a positive way.
3. Understand the nature of others and why they behave as they do.
4. Learn to manage relations with your staff, your colleagues, your stakeholders, clients, customers, the public, and any others that you may come into contact with. Be sensitive to their needs and wants as individuals. It is of critical importance to your continuing effectiveness as a manager.

Chapter 4:

Work/Life Balance

As managers and leaders, we must promote work/life balance, or our staff may become disenchanted, disengaged, and demoralized. I don't have to tell you that when staff are disenchanted, disengaged, and demoralized, the workplace culture becomes the antithesis of fun, and productivity suffers.

Work/life balance is also referred to as *work/life integration* and the terms can be used interchangeably. Regardless of what label is applied, for many, it has become the impossible dream. Almost every adult must spend 30 to 40 years in the workforce and close to one half of their waking hours at work. The other half of their waking life is spent looking after kids, parents, houses, spouses, religion, community, and every other possible need one can imagine without fail and without faltering.

In fact, as leaders, inspiring those around us to greater personal heights or higher levels of performance at work is becoming increasingly challenging, especially when we consider how increasingly complex work is becoming for many of us.

Let's look at the current reality.

- There are almost as many women in today's workforce as there are men. Sadly, the women are still most often responsible for looking after domestic issues, especially childrearing.
- Workers in every industry are being asked to accomplish more using fewer resources, often working more hours.
- Too many people are cancelling vacations, carrying them over, or asking that they be paid out. Collectively, we are not getting enough downtime.
- On March 8, 1996, the *Wall Street Journal* noted that 75 percent of those earning $100,000 or more annually reported that "managing time is a bigger problem than managing money."
- In 2008, a Desjardins Financial Security Survey entitled "Physical & Mental Health of Canadians" revealed that 74 percent felt overworked, 70 percent expected more depression and anxiety, 21 percent had more unscheduled days off to deal with personal stress than in 2000, and couples were working seven hours more per week than in 1976.
- Forty percent of American workers feel their jobs are not as important as they once were, with 70 percent reporting that most days felt like they would never end.
- Close to 40 percent of marriages today end in divorce, while 26 percent of families with children are single-parent families. Balancing the demands of home and work creates stress, and perhaps more disengaged staff.
- A headline from the *Globe and Mail*, October 31, 2010: "Our inability to balance jobs and home life is costing corporate Canada as much as $10 billion a year."

First, I would like to briefly consider what work/life balance really means. In order to properly consider this, we first need to consider what work/life balance may look like in an ideal world. This is the situation that occurs when an employee, the organization that employee works for, the employee's family, and the society within which the employee lives are all in complete harmony with one another. The result would be stress-free living.

However, there are 168 hours available to all of us each and every week of our lives—no more, no less. If we assume 8 hours per day are spent sleeping (I know for many of us that is only in our dreams), that leaves 112 hours a week for all our other activities—work, fun, eating, relaxing, etc. If 40 of these hours are spent at the workplace, we still have 72 for fun. So what's the problem?

The problem is that in 1900, people generally worked from dawn until dusk, at least six days a week, but they also had a life expectancy of fewer than fifty years, compared to today's expectancy of close to eighty years. Obviously, reducing work hours has been good for us. However, the issue here is not that we are working too many hours but that we are not confining our work to designated times. Rather, for many, work activities have begun to cross into our personal lives, while personal issues often intrude on our ability to perform effectively while at work.

An absolute dedication to the job and to our personal lives where neither one interferes with or disrupts the other may be an ideal that is not only unachievable now but may never have been achievable. We make it sound so simple. We have work as one part of our life, and everything else forms the rest of it. Therefore, if we just juggle these two elements, effectively employing a trick or two, balance, eternal bliss, and happiness are sure to follow. Remember that this describes an ideal situation, but consider if you will some of the following:

- For a large part of our world today, life is nothing more than a daily struggle for survival—there is no such thing as play time.
- For much of rural Canada and the United States, life in agriculture is not composed of tidy forty-hour-per-week segments. You do

what you must to make ends meet. Vacations and days off are pleasures only enjoyed by city folks.

- It may be noted that our parents and professionals in the 1950s would go home from work and not have cell phones, voice mail, e-mail, BlackBerries, etc., to continuously connect them to the workplace. However, they would still consider work problems while at home despite having a limited ability to act on those problems. Did they really always get the breaks that we thought they did?

- Also in the '50s, in many families, Father went to work while Mother looked after the house and the kids. Today, most families, in order to just enjoy a "reasonable" standard of living, must have both parents working outside the home. However, what is the definition of "reasonable"? When I was a child, there were nine of us living in a standard three-bedroom brick bungalow with only one bathroom (for a few years, until we moved into a huge four-bedroom two-story with one and a half baths—probably 1,400 square feet WOW!). "Reasonable" for many today is a minimum of 2,000 square feet with three bathrooms, a two-car garage, every electronic toy and gizmo known to exist, plus a cottage and at least two annual vacations to somewhere sunny and warm.

- Many parents today place incredible stress on themselves by placing kids in multiple sports or activities. These are not limited to neighbourhood park type games but include practice, games, competitions, and tournaments, many of which are not one-day events but involve something different every weekend. Occasionally they fret a bit and ask, "Where does the time go?" Gee, I wonder.

- The experts tell us we need 30 minutes of exercise daily. We should be at a ridiculously low BMI, which really means 30 minutes a day won't do it, and you can forget about those snacks you now enjoy. You also need at least 30 minutes a day in meditation. If we don't do 30 minutes, we get stressed out over it. To combat your stress levels and various forms of cancer, a glass of wine a day is good, but don't dare have two, or else! In addition, we need sunshine for vitamin D, but get too much and we risk skin cancer. How about daily vitamins? Omega 3-6-9? Vitamin E? Calcium? Magnesium? There is so much to do just to be healthy.

- Twenty-six percent of families in Canada are single-parent families. Their "balance" is the ability to pay the bills and keep food on the table all the while trying to keep the boss happy and the kids out of trouble. The same balance is faced by those on social assistance, the ones who are paid minimum wage, those who can find only temporary employment, or the 8 percent of the population that is unemployed.

- On the flipside of the coin, millions are well paid in their respective jobs but can't take work home with them. Or if overtime is needed, they are paid for it. These include unionized plant workers, nurses, firefighters, police officers, and health-care staff. For these folks, even if they can bring home with them physically, what about mentally and emotionally?

While work is not to blame—at least not 100 percent of the blame—is work adding to the complexity of our lives? I believe the answer is yes! Here's why I think so.

First, for those who are managers and others who are able to work from a virtual office, voice mail, e-mail, cell phones, and other such gadgets certainly make that "privilege" far more palatable. If I attend a conference all day, I am now able to work all evening too. Yippee! What a privilege that is. I can also take my BlackBerry on vacation and to the cottage so I can be that much more productive. Why not call folks while I'm grocery shopping or from the restaurant? No need to waste a minute of my time. Perpetual connectivity. While I understand that many folks are comfortable in this milieu, I am not convinced that it is a healthy situation. What I am convinced about is that many organizations try to take advantage of this comfort level by expecting that staff will be in touch with the workplace on a 24/7 basis.

Second, for the management teams of many organizations, the organizational culture seems to promote a competition to see who can work the most hours. If you're not putting in an extra 10 to 20 hours a week, you are clearly not dedicated enough. If you take your full allotment of vacation, there is something wrong. A truly great manager never has time for all of his or her vacation, right? Early mornings? Late evenings? Working lunches? Let's see who can do the most. Frankly, this starts at the top.

Tony Schwarz, in *The Way We're Working Isn't Working* (as reported by Wendy Le Leung in the *Globe and Mail*, June 1, 2010), notes, "Humans aren't meant to perform like computers, at high speed for long periods of time. If we routinely try to do so, we will be neglecting our four key needs—our physical needs, met through fitness, meditation and rest; our emotional need to feel valued; our mental need to control our attention; and our spiritual need to believe that what we do matters." Instead, what so often becomes the dominating theme of many organizations is the absolute, blind dedication to the workplace. I wonder if some of our headstones will say "I wish I had spent more time at the office"?

Third, we seem to have collectively developed a mindset that is fascinated with benchmarking and measuring. Let me note that I am not against measuring what we do. However, I see it more as our inducement to ask questions about operations and services with a view to bringing about improvements, as opposed to the dominant theme, which is centred around a desire to become increasingly more cost effective, producing more with fewer staff. The other terms that have become commonplace are *downsizing* and the more recent, politically correct *right sizing*. All this really means doing more with less. That attitude, in turn, means that those of us who are gainfully employed face a continuous demand on our time and energy to produce more and, when that happens, one way or another, it begins to intrude on our personal time and energy.

Fourth, I am the first one to say that it is important to always keep our customers' (or taxpayers for public sector employees) voices, needs, and wants foremost in our minds when making decisions. However, with the passage of time, customers and taxpayers are becoming more aware of their importance, and they are demanding more and wanting it sooner. In turn, the bosses (that includes all of us) are demanding more and wanting it sooner. The president has a great idea, so he tells the VP to get on it right away. Things are dropped, priorities shifted. Workloads are increased (with the implication of immediacy, of course), other projects are dropped, evenings and weekends are worked, and so it continues. The same thing happens in the public sector, where the mayor gets a call about an upcoming event that we should be supporting. His call goes to the city manager, who interrupts her work to listen and discuss with the appropriate director, who needs the input of five different staff people, who also have to change their schedules and workloads, with the result being that we are grossly inefficient. How difficult can it be to say no?

Fifth is the concept of "work creep." This is not about the guy in the cubicle next to you who gives you the wrong kind of goose bumps. I'm talking about our propensity to squeeze in a couple of more meetings, because, of course, there is no time left in our workday. So, in order to increase efficiency, we say, "How about breakfast? Won't work? Let's make it lunch." Perhaps just an occasional evening and the all-important weekend retreat. If we didn't have the breakfast meeting, where would we be? At home with our family (or at least the dog or cat for those who live alone). This creep doesn't happen all at once. It is insidious.

Finally, there is the concept of "team" at work. Make no mistake—that is a concept I promote. However, we talk about the work team being the one I spend at least five days a week with, for eight to ten hours a day. There is occasionally pressure from fellow employees to spend additional time with them, going for a drink after work or joining the company bowling team or going to the annual retreat or simply putting in extra time so the team can achieve better results. The problem is that this cuts into my personal life. When I finally get home, I hope to sleep for eight hours, which may leave as few as six hours for family or personal matters. Where do our priorities lie, with the work team or the family?

What Is the Front Line Saying?

In 2003, Dr. Linda Duxbury, Dr. Christopher Higgins, and Donna Coghill produced a study called "Voices of Canadians: Seeking Work-Life Balance," in which they surveyed 30,470 employees across Canada. A sampling of the comments captured by their study is reflected below. Do any of them sound familiar?

- "Flexible Hours" to some these days mean you can come in earlier and leave later and you can work through lunch.
- We are expected to do more with less.
- Is anyone listening to the employees? We doubt it.
- Our employees, supervisors, and company executive are unfocused, disengaged, and not on the same page, which, at times, results in a lot of extra work.
- My manager needs to recognize that I'm not out to screw my employer—they are my livelihood.
- There is still a tendency to look down on those employees who choose to respect the normal (paid) work day and leave to take care of family/home responsibilities.
- The people at the very top want the organization to appear to support family values. However, they put such strict production

expectations on the organization that the family values are the first to go by the wayside.

- If I need to take time off to balance my personal/work life, my work is piled up when I return.
- Constant changes in the workplace—many of which either seem unnecessary or have been arranged by those who are not in the front lines—add stress.(10)

Work/Life Conflict for Individuals

Let's be clear that many of those who are seeking the Holy Grail of work/life balance may be sadly disappointed. We all face troubling moments at home and at work. All we can really do for ourselves is to minimize the negative conflict and apportion our personal time and energy to work, and the rest of our lives, in a fashion that is productive and meaningful. There is no one perfect solution. We can't even blame a lack of money, believing that life would be perfect if only we were paid more or were independently wealthy because those who are wealthy also face their share of trials and tribulations, as evidenced by the litany of performers, athletes, and other newsworthy stars who seem to not take advantage of their fame and fortune, choosing instead to run afoul of common decency, morality, or even the law (just look at fallen stars such as Charlie Sheen, Barry Bonds, Lindsay Lohan, and Britney Spears).

The point is that we all to some degree face issues related to kids, parents, loss of lives, health, divorce, and cost of living. Sometimes there is just not enough time or energy to achieve everything we want to. At times, our job intrudes on our personal life, and at times our personal problems affect our ability to work. Housework and kids prevent us from taking time for ourselves. For millions, the long commute to work also takes its toll, robbing us of valuable time. We want to improve our education, but where do we find the time? For some, it's not about the job and life but rather the need to juggle two or more jobs to make ends meet. Is it all hopeless? Of course not, but there is no one, single, universal solution or magic potion that will lead us to a state of eternal bliss.

Attitude, Gratitude, Action

So much of this balance, or integration, comes back to our own attitude toward life. If balancing everything becomes such a huge burden that it threatens your health (or perhaps even your life), remember the words of a friend of mine, "Long time dead, so enjoy the short life you have," or as Robin Sharma says, "You don't want to be the richest person in the graveyard." Finally, as so many of us have seen elsewhere, and as I have already noted, we don't see many headstones that read "I wish I had spent more time at the office."

When I was younger, my parents would say, "Before you go out and play, clean up your room." "Before you can go fishing, the dishes need to be done." "If you want a new bike, you better continue delivering newspapers." When all was said and done, the lesson that I didn't appreciate at the time was simply that there is a time for work and a time for play. That was the way it was when I was a kid, and that is the way it should be now. Try not to confuse the two. Aim for good balance.

Juggling everything does not need to be a life sentence if you simply remember some key principles, most of which come down to your attitude. First, none of us needs to be all things to all people. We try diligently to be outstanding employees, parents, spouses, community members, and leaders, but sometimes we have to say no. Kids don't have to belong to every organization just because they exist or their friends belong to them or just because it seems like a good idea at the time. Tough love! Say no to some of it.

Second, make sure you enjoy what you do, and have fun at work. Doing something because it pays well is about the worst possible reason to stay at a job. Find work that you can be truly passionate about but work that also allows the balance that is so critical to all of us. Being passionate about your work to the point that it engages you 24/7 is not productive, not positive, and will not contribute to a meaningful balance in your life. We only have 24 hours a day to juggle our responsibilities and pleasures.

Third, look after yourself—physically, spiritually, emotionally, and mentally. In addition to your obligations with work and family, try to build some time into every day to read, meditate, reflect, rest, enjoy a massage, celebrate, enjoy nature, listen to music, or garden. Don't worry about doing all of them, but remember that it is doing just those things on occasion that truly make us happy. Remember all the things that make you smile or laugh, and try to do more of them.

Life does not always have to be a competition where "he who dies owing the most wins." We need to be thankful for what we have, especially in North America where we have so much to be thankful for. We have a wonderful standard of living, with outstanding health and educational systems. Most of us have good-paying jobs. A typical 1950s-style three-bedroom brick bungalow in the suburbs, which, by Canadian standards, is only marginally acceptable, would in many countries suggest a fairy-tale existence. We enjoy many freedoms, unheard of in so many parts of the world. Fresh air and clean, abundant water are also there for almost each and every one of us. Our basic needs are all but looked after, and yet so many believe there should be more. As Buddha is alleged to have said, "Let us rise up and be thankful for if we didn't learn a lot today, at least we learned a little, and if we didn't learn a little, at least we didn't get sick, and if we got sick, at least we didn't die. So let us all be thankful."

Instead of looking for more, let us be thankful for what we have, and if we are truly trying to make things better, let us at least turn our attention and energy to making life better for others. To do so requires that we turn our attention to my third key to achieving integration—action.

Every year, New Year's Eve brings a multitude of promises by almost every one of us to do something better—quit smoking, lose weight, exercise more, be better parents, and so on. The vast majority of those resolutions go unfulfilled. Most of us seem to appreciate that we need to achieve a reasonable balance between our work life and our personal life, but making it happen is an entirely different matter. We always have our reasons—not enough time or conflicting priorities. Perhaps we'll make changes next week or next month or next year. That isn't good enough. Start now.

If you want better work/life balance, you need to take action. Perhaps you could consider the following:

- Turn off your cell phone during the evenings and weekends.
- Take your vacation time but not your computer or cell phone.
- Remember that time you enjoy wasting sometimes may not be actually wasted.
- You don't need to be all things to all people, so don't try.
- It's okay to enjoy your work, but it's okay to enjoy your life too. Maybe you don't need the 4,000-square-foot house, plus the cottage in Muskoka, plus the yacht, plus the annual vacation to exotic destinations.
- Don't pay attention to the experts, TV shows, fashion magazines, or anything else that guides you to a life of perfection. Perfection is an illusion. Do your best to look after yourself physically, mentally, emotionally, and spiritually, but forget perfection. Don't get too stressed out because you don't have time to meditate for one hour every day or you can't squeeze in your daily 10k run—and can you imagine having two glasses of wine instead of just one? Do your best. Full stop.

What Can Organizations Do?

Let's start by walking the talk. Senior leaders must model the behaviour they desire from the rest of the staff. So many "speak from both sides of their mouths." In casual conversation, they are actually aware of the pressures faced by their staff. The information contained in this chapter is by no means new to them. Notwithstanding this knowledge, many organizational cultures evolve that almost seem to foster competition to see who works the most or who can put in the most overtime. As noted earlier in this chapter, often those who do their best to balance personal time and work time feel looked down upon, as if by doing so they are offending the integrity of the organization. It becomes easier to put in more work, dedicate less time to our personal lives, and so the cycle continues. What can we do?

First, management staff must be aware of the challenges associated with work/life balance and the implications of same for themselves, their staff, and the organization's ability to function. Staff who arrive for work shouldering personal concerns or problems are less focused, more likely to be disengaged, and possibly less productive. Hiring managers who are leaders with demonstrated interpersonal sensitivity would be a good start, but it doesn't end there. Awareness of the issues must be talked about within the organization. Training and development must be offered. Promoting a more relaxed work environment will not likely affect the bottom line at the expense of all else and will be in the best long-term interests of the organization. If staff feel that somebody understands their challenges and their manager is sensitive to the stress they are feeling, they will likely show up for work more regularly, and when they do, they will be more engaged and productive.

Second, managers need to know their staff as individuals. They are not simply human resources but real people with real lives and real problems that occupy their minds and their spirit, not just at home but also while at work. They are not machines that can turn off the personal mindset while at work and the work mindset while at home.

This doesn't mean a manager needs to socialize with staff, but she should be open to knowing them better. Communicate with them. Ask them about some of their non-work issues. Be sensitive to their stresses. Know that Jennifer went to her kids' concert last night or that John was playing in the league championship on the weekend or that Mabel just got back from Cancun. Ask them how these things worked out. We don't need to be intrusive, just sensitive and concerned.

Third, the organization needs to focus more attention on developing people skills in their managers. Forget technical training. This can be found in abundance for any profession. Managers need to become better communicators, be more adept at conflict management, and be better coaches and cheerleaders for their staff. If nothing else, they need to appreciate the simple importance of just being nice to each other.

Fourth, build organizational policies that support workplace flexibility and a general appreciation for work/life balance issues. Policies dealing with employee assistance programs, emergency leave provisions, vacation practices, limitations on overtime worked, as well as any others that recognize the sometimes conflicting lives that people lead.

Finally, for those who remain connected to the workplace via computer and cell phones, there needs to be an understanding that a 24/7 commitment to work is not realistic. There must be times when such devices are turned off. Nights, weekends, and vacations all need to become off limits. I am personally aware of some organizations that apply a "no computers" day on a regular basis. This forces staff to simply talk to one another. Interesting, isn't it?

Our only hope for any sense of balance in our lives is to develop the right attitude, combined with gratitude, for all that can be good (and there is plenty of good in the world), and we must, collectively, be prepared to take action!

Key Messages
Work/Life Balance

My father conveyed to me a dual message: "Always work hard, but always have something to look forward to that is fun, whether that be the weekend, vacation, or retirement." To that end I offer the following:

1. Our work should not be a competition to see who can work the hardest or work the most overtime. If you need to put in that much overtime, clearly you are doing something wrong.
2. Maintain a healthy attitude toward life and toward work. Work hard, play hard, and don't try to be all things to all people. Just do your best.
3. Be thankful for the wonderful things we do have. So many of us enjoy good health, an excellent education system, an overall good standard of living, interesting and well-paying jobs, good friends, and families that love us and support us. Appreciate it all.
4. If you want to improve your work/life balance, then do something about it. Stop whining and take appropriate action.

Chapter 5:

Silos and Organizational Constipation

For most of us, we don't approach work as a means to another end. While paying the bills is important, most of us will spend 40 years of our lives at work; it is as natural for us as so many other institutions and aspects of our lives. We live, we learn, we grow up, we get married, we have families, we are a part of the community, and we work! Therefore, let us understand as much about the workplace as we possibly can so that we can enjoy going to work more and, as managers, help our staff be more productive when at work.

When we were young, most of us were taught about proper conduct and the importance of following certain rules. For example, we all know that it's not right to steal. We were also taught that we must not lie or cheat or abuse other people or animals. In fact, regardless of our religious leanings (or lack thereof), some variation of the Ten Commandments has been passed on to most of us. The point is that we all eventually develop a personal code of values that we live by. It may not be written, and we may not take time to properly reflect on that code as often as we should, but it exists nonetheless.

Organizations are no different. They too have a set of values and, like most of us, they don't spend enough time reflecting on those values, talking about them, promoting them, or even ensuring adherence to them. Ultimately, the values that we, as individuals, grow up with and enter the workforce with may not always be the same as those espoused by our workplaces.

So why is it that so many organizational managers and leaders are so focused on making money, making widgets, building bridges or selling cars that they forget the importance of their own culture and their own people? This is not touchy-feely HR fluff. In *Built to Last,* Jim Collins reflected on what exactly great companies have done to ensure themselves of continuing success. "[Great companies] build an organization that fervently preserves its core ideology in specific, concrete ways. The visionary companies translate their ideologies into tangible mechanisms aligned to send a consistent set of reinforcing signals. They indoctrinate people, impose tightness of fit, and create a sense of belonging to something special."(11)

The most important thing is to ensure that the staff members an organization hires and manages reflect the same values and principles. Everyone believing in the big picture will assist the departments in achieving their own goals, resulting in staff that are engaged and productive. Notwithstanding what Collins has discovered and written about, so many individuals and so many organizations just don't get it. So why do we care about organizational culture in the first place, and if we do understand it better, how can that improve the work lives of all of us?

Organization Defined

An organization is merely a collection of people who come together to achieve some common purpose, be it selling widgets, delivering services to taxpayers, or any other business venture. Theoretically, within that organization, there will be some common understanding, by all the players involved, about what their respective roles are and how those roles combine for the common good. For many of the organizational players, the roles involve the creation of rules, policies, and procedures, to ensure efficiency of operations and consistency of application. These support services, such as finance, purchasing, legal, HR, risk management, and IT have a role to perform to support operations and provide appropriate advice, counsel, and guidance. Operational departments deliver their services directly to the customer. Each has a role to play, not as individuals but as departments. Ultimately, this is the very essence of an organization—the coming together of many to act as one.

Organizations evolve over time, and through that evolution, they develop their own unique personality with the stories that people tell of it, both good and bad, but stories that contribute meaningfully to its history and personality. Difficult times and challenges have been overcome and have made the organization stronger, more resilient. Let us remember that, as individuals, our personalities are determined in much the same way (though psychologists have not yet fully settled the question of nature versus nurture). We have our own unique DNA, experiences, challenges, histories, and qualities that will take us where we want to go.

Unfortunately, we often think of an organization as an entity or a thing and so, our inclination is to not attach a personality or cultural measure to it. In reality, an organization is a living, breathing, dynamic unit, and for each us to be an inspiring part of that unit and to contribute in a meaningful fashion to it, we need to know more about its culture.

Dysfunctional Organizational Culture

I enjoy and appreciate Scott Adams's portrayal of a workplace culture through his *Dilbert* cartoons. For those who don't know, Dilbert is the engineer who appears technically sound, socially pathetic, and frustrated beyond comprehension by organizational characters, such as the pointy-haired boss who is grossly inefficient and ineffective,

Wally the perpetual malingerer, Alice the intimidator, as well as a cast of other unique characters that all of us may have faced at work one time or another.

Adams offers his own description in the introduction to his book *This Is the Part Where You Pretend to Add Value*: "You might have noticed that corporations hum along no matter who is sick, vacationing, or recently dead. Any one person's value on any particular day is vanishingly small. The key to career advancement is appearing valuable despite all hard evidence to the contrary. If you pretend well enough, you can become CEO."(12) Combined with this description, on a daily basis, we see a multitude of jokes about organizational ineptitude. Are the following perhaps vaguely familiar?

1. Allegedly, a company memo from HR states the following: Our company does not require any fitness program! We get enough exercise running down the boss, climbing to the top, chasing down rumours, stabbing each other in the back, dodging responsibility, and pushing our luck.
2. In a Dilbert cartoon, a group is about to commence a meeting with the comment "I would like to open this meeting by assigning blame for its eventual failure."
3. Even Red Green gets into the act in his book *How to Do Everything*. In it he has a section on how to survive an office job with tips on doing just enough not to get fired but not enough to be given any responsibility. He recommends looking for a "disorganized management regime where nobody really knows who does what or how anything gets done." He also gives tips on how to look busy without really doing anything, creating the perception of competence while avoiding commitment, keeping a messy desk, encouraging telemarketers to call you at work to give a perception of being busy and, ultimately, looking for "a Canadian raise—the same pay for less work."(13)

Why the cynicism about our organizations? Could it be that where there's smoke, there's fire? For the managers and leaders out there, how many of our staff are coming to work because they have to, because it's a means to an end, a way to pay the bills? How many employees show up at work and just go through the motions? We get a service award that essentially proclaims that we survived 25 or 30 years of service. For some who go through their work lives like this, it is a serious waste of time and a waste of life. Why shouldn't we all be proud of our respective workplaces? Why can't we all go out and brag about the fun we have at work and how wonderful and great and efficient everything is? Why do we so often look for and find the flaws rather than seek out and revel in the benefits that organizations have to offer?

Simply put, we don't, as organizations, spend enough time or energy promoting our core ideologies and values. Nor do we spend sufficient energy aligning people in our employ with these ideologies and values. As a result, far too often, departments/divisions follow the beat of their own drummers, the result being there is no organizational culture or personality. Alternatively, it could be argued that some organizational cultures are really just a patchwork of the respective departments' cultures contained therein. This leads to one of the most prevalent concerns in modern organizations, the lack of one unifying culture, replaced instead by a series of subcultures that may or may not contribute meaningfully to one overall theme.

Mission, Vision, and Values

There is nothing wrong, contrary to what we read in *Dilbert*, with organizational missions, visions, and values. I do have a concern, however, that all too often we craft them because it is politically correct to do so. In those instances, missions, visions, and values become nothing more than words on paper. However, with the right spirit, intent, and follow-through, organizational mission, vision, and values may at least negate the formation of silos and even encourage a healthy, fun, and productive workplace. There will be less of a focus on independent departments and a greater focus on the organization as a whole.

As individuals, we live our lives and make decisions based on a set of values; however, for the most part, we never stop to consider what those values are or spend any time identifying them. They are often values that are drilled into us by parents, teachers, and others, who have been particularly inspirational for us. Again, quoting Jim Collins from *Built To Last,* visionary companies "[do not] rise to greatness because they wrote one of the vision, values, purpose, mission, or aspiration statements that have become popular in management today (although they wrote such statements more frequently than the comparison companies and decades before it became fashionable).Creating a statement can be a helpful step in building a visionary company, but it is only one of thousands of steps in a never-ending process of expressing the fundamental characteristics we identified across the visionary companies."(14) I have said about leadership that it is not some kind of birthright. Nor does it come with a title. It is defined by one's actions. So it is with missions, visions, and values. Our organizational culture comes not from what we write on paper but how, over the years, and through countless situations, we conduct ourselves. It may include written statements, but more importantly it reflects unstated values, customs, rituals, behavioural expectations, stories, language, and an understanding that, especially as an organization grows, more than a single culture is bound to evolve. While it may be true that silos will never be totally eradicated, if we fail to address the issues related to silos as they arise, we can be certain that they will continue to thrive. Leadership must continuously promote the good of the organization over the good of any one department. Organizations can encourage creativity and innovation but only where it contributes meaningfully to the overall good of the organization.

Silos and Organizational Constipation

In his book *Silos, Politics, and Turf Wars,* Patrick Lencioni defines silos as "nothing more than the barriers that exist between departments within an organization, causing people who are supposed to be on the same team to work against one another. And whether we call this phenomenon departmental politics, divisional rivalry, or turf warfare, it is one of the most frustrating aspects of life in any sizable organization."(15)

I would like to take this issue one step further. Silos exist in every organization and are really the result of departments or services that sometimes fail or forget to acknowledge that they are part of a larger entity. Instead of ensuring that their goals, visions, and values align with that larger entity, they begin to view their service as an island unto itself. The result is the simple lack of promotion of the good of the organization as a whole and the possibility that ten different departments are travelling in ten different directions.

A further point of frustration for many is support departments, whose very purpose is to provide support, advice, and guidance to operating departments. I noted earlier who the culprits are—finance, purchasing, risk management, PR, marketing, legal, and yes, even HR (which may explain why Adams reserves a special place in his cartoons for Catbert, the evil director of HR).

At this point, I need to be very clear, lest my colleagues over the years, from various support departments, come to believe I have suddenly abandoned them. As noted in my definition of the organization, there must be a common goal or purpose, and what often ties apparently disparate parts of an organization together is the support services. They have an incredibly important role to play in ensuring consistency, providing service, and protecting against a host of potential pitfalls and pratfalls in addressing day-to-day business activities.

However, my concern has been that many of these services often take their role to a point above and beyond that which they are intended to play, applying rules and policies so rigidly that they soon stifle energy, enthusiasm, and the creative spirit that may otherwise be found in each and every one of us. Support departments establish their own culture, while operating departments soon begin to devise unique ways and means of avoiding the rules and policies. That practice, in turn, leads to a further fracturing of what should be a single, unifying organizational culture.

As someone once said, "Organization is the enemy of improvisation." Support departments reflect the epitome of organization. They cause organizational constipation, a situation where members of the organization become paralyzed by the fear of trying anything out of the ordinary simply because there is a cadre of policies or rules intended to protect or guide them but which are ultimately interpreted so as to block them at every possible turn.

General Rick Hillier, in his book *Leadership*, notes, "Excessive processes don't inspire people to excel, and they don't work as a replacement for a strategic approach or for building a network of people."(16) Well intended but remarkably frustrating. So what can we do? First, for the employees of those support services, always remember that your primary role is to offer support, counsel, and guidance. You are there to help others do their jobs better. You are not there to control or limit them. Second, if you are a member of an operating department, remember to heed the advice of your colleagues in the support areas, and remember that they are there to help, not hinder you. Hard to believe, but it's true.

Why Silos Continue to Exist

Silos exist because there is often no good, obvious reason to work together. There is no common goal that is known and pursued by all. In order to eliminate the silos, the organization must have a single, energizing, unifying raison d'être. In essence, that is why we partake in our retreats and do our strategic planning. We need to create mission, vision, and values. As my father used to say, "Talk is cheap." We need to move beyond the creation of the mission, vision, and values, refusing to merely put the words on paper and choosing instead to practise what we preach. The unifying culture is the result of actions, which, as we all know, speak louder than words.

Organizational Politics

Silos and subcultures are a reality. Organizational politics are also a reality. Remember that the culture of the organization is its personality and the actions it has taken, collectively, over the years, with its stories, its history, its successes, and its failures. Politics and the struggles between departments and individuals help form that culture.

It is truly all about how different departments conduct their activities and how their actions, in turn, positively or negatively affect other departments, services, and clients. It becomes important information for individuals who have to work with others and may be frustrated by what Lencioni calls "the daily pain of departmental politics as they are left to fight bloody, unwinnable battles with their colleagues."(17)

Politics exist in every organization, the only variable being the nature of the organizational leadership and their ability to rise above petty politics to focus on the best interests of the organization as a whole. In the meantime, as part of the organization, we all need to accept that politics will exist and then determine who has what power and how to take best advantage of that knowledge.

My favourite example of this approach involves those strange bedfellows, HR and finance. Over the years, many of my colleagues in finance have seemed to lacked the sensitivity to people issues that HR folks are noted for. Similarly, the HR staff often fail to grasp the nuances of budget or financial control. When starting in a new organization, I will immediately build solid relations with the director/VP of finance, with the promise that I will look after her people issues in exchange for an assurance that she will look after my money issues. HR staff will subsequently suggest that I'm too soft with the finance department, choosing to give them too much latitude with HR matters. However, if, in exchange, I can garner support for my budget or spending initiatives, that latitude will have been worthwhile. That's how to use organizational politics to your advantage. Too many departments are bound to have their own way, showing finance or HR who is in charge. It serves nobody's best interests to establish these turf wars. Use the players to full advantage.

There will always be some players in the organization who have devoted a great deal of time and energy to create the systems that currently exist. The older the organization, the more evident this is. As a result, they are not fond of others suggesting that changes may be warranted. It's comfortable the way it is, thank you very much, and suggesting change is needed a threat to their investment in the organization. To quote Charles Sorenson, "It isn't the incompetent who destroy our organization. It is those who have achieved something and want to rest upon their achievements who are forever clogging things up." If you believe change is needed in your organization, be prepared. It will never be easy and will most assuredly come with its share of pain and upset. Change is never easy, but without change there would be no butterflies.

How Do We Measure the Culture of an Organization?

So far, I haven't painted a rosy picture of organizational life—silos, politics, resistance to change; generally a cynical outlook. However, there is always hope, and while organizational life can often range between being a joke and a royal pain in the ass, organizations also can achieve great things along the way. So what does a good organizational culture look like? How do we measure it? Obviously, one of the measures of a good culture is whether the organization achieves anything. Is it doing what it set out to do? Is it producing? Also, is it contributing meaningfully to society as a whole? Are staff excited to be part of it? Is the work environment safe? Is it stable? Does it have a sense of where it has been and where it is going (because if we don't know where we are going, any road will get us there).

Every year in Canada, as in most countries, there are numerous employer competitions to determine the top 100, top 50, etc. One of the leaders in these competitions is Mediacorp's sponsorship of Canada's Top 100 Employers. The editors select the top 100 from more than 2,000 applications each year and then examine eight key criteria: (1) physical workplace; (2) work atmosphere and social; (3) health, financial, and family benefits; (4) vacation and time off; (5) employee communications; (6) performance management; (7) training and skills development; and (8) community involvement. These are the criteria examined by the judges, but what do they really tell us?

The applications submitted in these competitions often sound good, but they do reveal an accurate reflection of the workplace? Staff create an application that spans hundreds of pages expounding just how great they are. However, I am also aware of numerous cases where the staff at these "top" organizations tell a much different story. I am not suggesting that applicants lie or even exaggerate the truth. However, those with great writing skills or those who best know how to paint a great picture that portrays their organization in the best possible light are those who are most likely to be successful.

Employer competitions portray one picture, but another measure and perhaps one that is more meaningful involves an examination of workplaces where the picture is not quite so rosy. Christine Pearson and Christine Porath, in their book *The Cost of Bad Behaviour*, reflect on their research, which not only demonstrates the incredible prevalence of incidents of incivility and disrespect in the workplace but also points to a huge cost to the US economy. In 2005, this cost of incivility was estimated by Pearson and Porath to be more than $300 billion, with 365 million work days lost each year due to on-the-job stress, $220 billion worldwide per year for treatment, and 40 percent of the US workforce affected by stress each year. Stress-related disability claims are the fastest growing category of claims in North America and Europe, with more than 1.5 times the number of claims that were submitted for physical injuries.(18) Readers who may be disinclined to buy into the theoretical perspectives espoused by these researchers and authors can choose, instead, to accept my word, based on anecdotal evidence accumulated over 40 years and hundreds of exit interviews. We attract staff to our organizations with pay, benefits, and reputation—all three must be competitive. However, once on board, we retain staff with a positive culture, solid management practices, and a respectful work environment, together with opportunities for growth and development. With all the exit interviews we have conducted over the years, it is almost never the case that staff leave for more money.

So, if lack of respect and incivility are the hallmarks of a bad organizational culture, what are the measures of a positive culture? I don't need to reinvent the wheel. Graham Lowe says it best in his *Creating Healthy Organizations*, where he describes a healthy culture as follows:

> The biggest difference between healthy and unhealthy cultures is their values. Healthy organizations value respect, responsibility, honesty, fairness, and integrity. Indeed, these are the qualities most people want in any relationship. The power of these values lies in how they influence day-to-day interactions among co-workers; between managers and employees; between employees and their customers or clients, suppliers, and business partners; and between the organization and the larger community. The result is a positive upward spiral of improved quality of work life and performance.(19)

I would make one addition to this description: Does the organization apply those values to the interactions between managers or between departments? The point remains that we must aim for an improved quality of work life, which leads invariably to engaged staff. Engaged staff are focused and happy staff. They feel respected and needed, properly recognized, and rewarded. Another means of determining if you have engaged staff is to receive an unequivocal yes to the following questions:

- Do I know what is expected of me in my job?
- Do I have the right tools, equipment, and communications?
- Does my boss know me as an individual?
- Do I have the opportunity to do what I do best?
- Am I recognized and appreciated?
- Does my employer spend time, energy, and money to develop me?
- Is my opinion counted? Is it important?
- Are we all committed to quality?

In addition, an organization can do a number of things to create and maintain outstanding departments, which will lead to an engaged staff:

- Orientation and training, emphasizing values, norms, history, and tradition. So often, in tight budgetary times, development and education dollars are slashed. Get the good staff first and don't forget to dedicate time and resources to their continuing development.
- On-the-job socialization. Don't use a "sink-or-swim" philosophy for new staff. Allow them time to get to know their colleagues.
- Practices encouraging promotion from within. New blood is occasionally needed, but staff want to know that if they work

hard and are dedicated and loyal, there may be rewards for them in the future. It helps also to maintain the culture.

- Sharing of good news with all staff. If someone in the department receives a letter of commendation from satisfied customers or other such good news, share it with everyone, but try not to embarrass the star. Knowing your employees as individuals will help you decide what to share, when, and how.
- A unique language and terminology that can set the organization apart from others, in the same way that Disney refers to their staff as "cast members." Make it realistic, but consider this as an option.
- Corporate songs, pledges, and affirmations that staff will buy into.
- Awards, contests, and public recognition events. Again, these have to be meaningful for the staff involved. This can be done at an annual awards luncheon, via newsletters, or at other important staff get-togethers. Contests can be held to encourage staff to submit new ideas for products or approaches that save money.
- Tolerance for honest mistakes, following the old adage that if we risk nothing we risk everything.
- Continuous focus on values and being part of something special. Your staff will get you where you want to go. In fact, you can't do it without them, so treat them right.

Attitude

Creating a great place to work depends on great attitudes. Senior leaders must work as a team with the best interests of the organization at the root of everything they do and every decision they make. Decisions cannot be self-serving. Managers must promote a work environment that is respectful and fosters absolute employee engagement. Staff is obligated to be enthusiastic, positive, and respectful of one another, wanting to do the very best job possible. If we can't approach work in this fashion, it is time to move on and bless some other employer with our presence. We can always teach skills, but what we can't teach is attitude.

Key Messages
Organizational Culture

The Bible had Ten Commandments, and most major religions have similar value statements to guide us to proper conduct. Between our religious education and our parents, these very important messages were constantly drilled into our heads. In turn, they formed the basis of our own "house rules," as well as a family culture. The organizations we work for are no different.

1. The support departments need to remember their role, which is to support the operating departments and their staff. We exist to serve them, not the other way around.
2. Organizational culture comes not only from our missions, visions, and values but more importantly from consistency of actions taken over time. It's all right to have these documents, but they must be supported and demonstrated by all staff, who must walk the talk.
3. We all need to come to work with the right attitude, and we must hire people with the right approach to work. Ultimately, we can teach skills, but we can't teach attitude.

Chapter 6:

Let's Have Fun

On occasion, the media will explore a famous person's life story, and in the course of that exploration, we hear said famous person say something like, "How can I complain? I get paid huge sums of money to do something that is so much fun." It is probably fair to suggest that most of us don't get paid "huge sums of money" whether we have fun or not. As a result, as long as we receive what we perceive to be a reasonable compensation package, our focus needs to switch to having as much fun as possible while we are there. For those of you who have had several jobs over the course of your career, if you were to ponder which job you considered your favourite, would the selection be based upon the pay level? The level of productivity you enjoyed? How efficiently you were able to work? Or perhaps it was the one that was the most fun? We all know which answer is the right one.

Even speaking anecdotally, the most obvious benefit of having fun or just being able to exercise a good sense of humour is that it results in better performance, increased creativity, and more productivity, with an overall increase in job satisfaction. Employees who are more engaged (measured by factors such as having more fun, enjoying their work, feeling challenged, appreciated, and respected) will suffer lower stress levels and enjoy more regular attendance. This simple factor is important enough that some progressive organizations are starting to include the promotion of fun as one of their core values.

If I achieve nothing else through the writing of this book, I hope that I can convince the reader that the most important element of any job—and any career decision you make—is that you must enjoy what you do, almost to the point that you are having fun at work. The simple reality is that if you're not having fun at work, there is something dramatically wrong and it's time for a change. The same applies to all your staff. To quote Tom Peters, "If you are not working for a company that is enthusiastic, energetic, creative, curious and just plain fun; you are in trouble! ... Serious trouble."(20) There are many who would have us believe that work is not meant to be fun but is meant to be work, and for some reason we must keep the two separate and distinct. However, having fun at work does not mean becoming unproductive or unprofessional.

Before we go any further, it may be prudent to dispel some myths about having fun and enjoying a good sense of humour while at work.

1. Myth: Work is no place for fun.
    An old school of thought was that work is serious business where fun has no place. However, it may be that fun at work is possible when the nature of the workplace is such that it invites a degree of "playful professionalism." "Fun*cilitators," the organization led by Gail Howerton, or even a high-tech organization like Google are known for their approach to work, their creativity, and the fun they seek on a daily basis. Surely, an organization as disciplined as the Canadian Armed Forces would not promote it. And yet, in General Rick Hillier's recent book *Leadership,* he notes, "Humour is powerful and one of the best tools available for your team, and also for you personally. When you can smile, the keys of office do not seem so heavy."(21)

A good sense of humour can lead to good fun, and both are possible in the workplace. The precision and tension so commonplace in a high-stress organization, such as the Boston Philharmonic Orchestra, does not seem conducive to having fun. Yet Benjamin Zander, conductor of that orchestra, in his book *The Art of Possibility*, notes, "Humour and laughter are perhaps the best way we can 'get over ourselves.' Humour can bring us together around our inescapable foibles, confusions, and miscommunications, and especially over the ways in which we find ourselves acting entitled and demanding, or putting other people down, or flying at each other's throats."(22) No matter what the nature of your workplace, a good sense of humour is important, and it's certainly okay to have fun. It may be the only way to enjoy what you do.

2. Myth: Laughter equals "goofing off."
    As with all things, balance is the key. There is a time and a place for everything, and while I am the first to promote fun and laughter at work, I am somewhat less enthusiastic about, for instance, a fire crew laughing their way through a five-alarm blaze or a surgical team chuckling while performing a delicate surgical procedure (especially when I'm the one under the scalpel). However, in most cases, more fun equates to more engaged and enthusiastic staff and a stronger sense of "team." Laughter and fun at the right time is the furthest thing one could imagine from "goofing off."

3. Myth: Workplace fun will lead to harassment complaints.
    In the same vein as the "goofing off" myth above, there is a time and a place for everything. Fun and humour must be appropriate, not enjoyed at the expense of colleagues or others. Having fun at work does not need to bring harassment complaints or human rights charges with it. Common sense must define our character and our way of doing business and

the culture of every organization must continue to reflect appropriate conduct on the part of all members in all of their activities.

4. Myth: Having fun is a waste of time.
    Nonsense! While there seems to be no good reason that we shouldn't aim to have as much fun as possible in life, can we at least promote it as a good business practice? The answer is clearly yes, and there are several benefits to this approach, discussed below.

- **It's good for our health.** If you're having fun at work, how does it feel? Great, doesn't it? Have a good healthy laugh and then look at yourself in the mirror. You are relaxed, smiling, and generally look great. Look at someone who is under a great deal of stress and you'll see the exact opposite. They are drained, ashen, and looking run down. Fun reduces stress. When was the last time you heard of someone having a heart attack following a good laugh? If you had your preferences, would you take a dose of cod liver oil or just have a good laugh? If we are having fun, we tend to be healthier, and if we are healthier, we are more productive and are a greater pleasure to have as part of the team and part of the organization. While I can't personally guarantee you will live longer by having fun and maintaining a good sense of humour, I can guarantee that your life will be less stressful and it will feel a lot better.
- **But what about absenteeism?** In this regard, I would invite readers to perform a simple study of your own organization. Review the attendance records and history of various departments. I'm willing to bet that those divisions or departments that have the most fun also have the lowest absenteeism rates. These departments may emphasize more than just fun. They may focus equally on respecting and appreciating staff, and therefore the reality is that employees

who are happiest attending work (perhaps because they have the most fun) will have the best attendance records. Let's be honest. We all have days when we don't feel 100 percent healthy and we must decide whether to drag ourselves out of bed and go to work or call in sick. It may be a bit of a cold, sore throat, a migraine, or a case of "40 oz. flu." If we feel respected, appreciated, and an important part of the team and we generally have fun at work, we will show up. If not; we don't. We call the boss and say we can't make it today. Similarly, for a medical procedure, when our physician says to stay off work for four to six weeks, if we have fun at work, we try to convince the doc that we're ready to go back after three. If not, we try to negotiate a couple of extra weeks off. Add this sort of attitude up for the entire organization and having a fun workplace may just make a significant difference in the cost of your absenteeism. While a solid work ethic may help drive great departments, I respectfully submit that, more likely, a "fun" atmosphere encourages more regular attendance of all staff.

- **Staff are more engaged.** There are immense benefits to organizations that promote employees having fun at work. In an article written by Lisa Belkin in the March 6, 2008, edition of the *New York Times*, Ms. Belkin notes the following:

> Being fun gets you hired. A study of 737 chief executives of major corporations found that 98 percent would hire an applicant with a good sense of humor over one who seemed to lack one.

> Having fun at work makes people loyal! According to a survey of 1,000 workers conducted for the authors by the research firm Ipsos, employees who laugh at work tend to stay. Those who rated their manager's sense of humor "above average" also said there was a 90 percent chance they would stay in their job for more than a

year. If they worked for a boss whose sense of humor they describe as "average" or below, the employee's chances of staying dropped to 77 percent.

Amusing people go far! According to a study in the *Harvard Business Review*, executives described by co-workers as having a good sense of humour "climb the corporate ladder more quickly, and earn more money than their peers."

A good laugh is good for your health! It increases blood flow and just makes us feel better. We know staff are fully engaged in their work if they can answer the questions in chapter 5 with a yes.

- **Turnover decreases.** Have fun at work and you're less likely to be interested in leaving your current employer to work elsewhere. While this may not be the only factor that affects staff turnover, it is certainly a major one. I have conducted many exit interviews, and it has been my experience that the clear majority of terminating employees do so because they feel unappreciated or disrespected; or that the workplace is unacceptable, uncaring, or just not fun. They terminate employment because of poor relationships, poor development opportunities, and poor coaching from the boss. The biggest complaints we so often hear from frontline managers is that staff recruitment activities take too long, do not produce guaranteed results, and adversely affect the ongoing performance of the department. If that is the case, make sure your staff stay with you. Experts project the cost of replacing staff to be two to three times the annual salary of the position being filled. What on earth can be done to stop the bleeding? Keep your staff engaged, happy, and having fun. If you can ensure that your staff have fun, you will dramatically increase the odds of retaining staff, reducing absenteeism, having a more productive staff, and in the end you and your staff will be less stressed and healthier.

What Managers Can Do

As a manager, you can take actions to help make work more fun for you and your staff. While we covered some of these in the chapter on work/life balance (and will cover more when we deal with alternative work arrangements), let's discuss some more here. Consider any or all of the following:

- Be more flexible in work start and finish times. Understand that staff have personal challenges and issues that need to be addressed. Flexibility is critical for a manager. Be understanding and be compassionate.
- Compressed work weeks are no longer considered to be a type of leading edge employee relations approach. While a manager must always remember the terms of the collective agreements that he/she may be subject to, think outside the box (my God, that's an overworked expression—it's almost as bad as telling someone to use common sense) and consider letting staff work four 10-hour days instead of five 8-hour days. Why not? If the job still gets done and staff are happier, why should we care?
- What about job sharing or part-time work? Two staff members may be able to share one job for either a temporary period (to help raise kids, look after sick or dying relatives, take a break from work, go back to school, etc.), or it may even be considered as a permanent arrangement. Why do we always insist on full time only? Not everybody necessarily wants or needs full-time work. Be flexible.
- What about telecommuting, virtual offices, or just doing some work from home? While there may be challenges with these programs and they may not be suitable for all employees or for every job in the organization, keep your mind open to new possibilities. It doesn't have to be permanent or even five

days a week, but on an occasional basis it can prove workable and beneficial for both the staff members who may need the flexibility as well as for the organization.

It's All about Attitude and Approach

I have now successfully spent close to 40 years in the workplace, managing and leading others, observing those practices that have been both successful and not so successful. In addition, I have spent a significant amount of time reading about leadership, writing about it, interviewing top organizational leaders to understand their secrets, and giving presentations on the topic, and I have really come to the inescapable conclusion that having fun at work is no different from having fun while away from work. It's all a matter of the right attitude and the right approach.

Many of those whom I interviewed for my first book had no idea what they did specifically, and indeed they struggled to define what fun at work meant to them or their teams. They just knew that they all enjoyed coming to work, and when pressed, time and time again, the word *attitude* was the one that they came back with most often.

We all know of folks who see the glass as half full and those who see the glass as half empty. Which are you? As I explained in *Common Sense Leadership*, I had occasion earlier in my career to go to lunch every week with a couple of colleagues who tended to drift into conversations about how horrible and pathetic the state of the world was in. Invariably, they could find a host of examples of world events that supported their negative views. For those one-hour periods each week, my glass tended to become half empty, and my mood consistently reflected same. That's how it seems with some people. A common refrain from them was, "If it weren't for bad luck, I wouldn't have any luck at all." However, I once had a message hanging in my office that said,

Everybody brings happiness into this office;
some when they enter;
others when they leave.

Regardless of the mood, disposition, or concerns of people visiting my office, I try to find a reason to be happy. Some folks are just like that. They are the ones who always have a smile on their face and a song in their heart. As an employer, a manager, and an organizational leader over the years, I would rather these people on my team than those who are more technically competent but no fun to be with or perpetually negative. As General Hillier noted,

People work better, think better, and relate to others better when they are happy and buoyant than they do when they are sad, troubled, insecure or cynical. What you do as a leader can have a tremendous effect on that. Just think about it: if you walk down the street and smile at ten people walking toward you, nine will likely smile back ... all too often in Canada we look at the silver lining in the clouds that cover our skies and search until we find its small, dark lining and then focus on that dark lining to the exclusion of all else. In fact, many of us tend to focus on it until we become cantankerous and pessimistic.(23)

As one of the interviewees from my first book told me, "You can't train attitude." However, there are five things you can do.

- Enjoy what you do.
- Focus on solutions not problems.
- Keep yourself and others positive.
- Help people laugh.
- Keep things in perspective.

1. Enjoy what you do

As I have noted previously, most of us will spend somewhere close to 40 years of our lives in the workplace. I cannot imagine anything more wasteful than not enjoying what you are doing for the bulk of those years. Granted, some phases of our work life may be less enjoyable than others. However, it remains critical that you take pride in what you do, be completely satisfied with your career, and for the most part have fun doing it. Miserable staff, managers, and leaders are not a good fit for anyone in any organization. We need engaged staff who are focused and happy. We want them to come to work looking forward to the experience. Regardless of your role in the organization, you must enjoy what you are doing. If you don't, it is time to step down, step out, or make some other essential changes to your job, your role, or your life in general.

Sadly, according to the Conference Board of Canada, employee job satisfaction plummeted from 61 percent in 1987 to 45 percent in 2009. During the same period, those who found their work interesting dropped from 70 percent to 51 percent. This is unacceptable. What has led us to this state of affairs? We must all get our priorities in order. We worry too much about making money for ourselves and the company to impress the kids, the neighbours, or just ourselves. Also, we need to get back to the basics. If we have more fun at work, even if it means less money, our lives will ultimately be much richer. As Will Rogers once said, "Too many people spend money they haven't earned to buy things they don't need to impress people they don't like." Maintain the proper perspective.

Leaders and managers need to ensure that we have the right people for the organization. There must be a good fit, and when they're there, they must be doing a good job. There is a strong likelihood that if you're not having fun at work, you are not a good fit for the organization or the organization is not a good fit for you. That happens. If you continue to pursue a career or a job solely for the money or because somebody else thinks it's a good thing to do, the stress you cause yourself and others may become unbearable. Not only will you suffer, but your family, friends, and staff will suffer with you. So examine what you are doing and make sure you enjoy doing it.

2. Focus on solutions, not problems

When I was a young manager, one of my bosses would often say, "Bring me solutions, not problems." Most of us have likely heard a similar refrain from some mentor or supervisor in our lives. But what does this really mean?

- First, this will only work in an environment of trust. As your coach and manager, I expect you to do your job. I don't want you in your job if you don't have the skills and abilities to do it. In addition, if you are bringing me problems to solve on your behalf, it suggests that there are two of us doing the job that one person is supposed to be doing. If that is the case, one of us needs to go.
- Second, if I am doing a good job of coaching and leading my employees, I will be encouraging them to use their minds and their natural talents to think their way through any problem placed before them. As a result, I expect them (and so should you) to think things through before coming to me and to be using me as a sounding board to refine solutions that they present.
- Finally, as an employee, I want to make myself indispensable to the department and the organization. By focusing on solutions and not whining about problems that I face, I make myself far more fun to be with and to be managed. If we all take that approach, our collective bosses will not want to lose us. It's a matter of self-preservation.

3. Keep yourself and others positive

I have said it repeatedly: "It's all about attitude." You are a manager and you are a leader. No matter what troubles may befall you, your people look to you to be positive and upbeat, and frankly you need them to be the same. Negative thinking is a disease, like an infection, and once it takes hold of your mind, it continues to grow. We can no longer see the forest for the trees and all thoughts become negative. We stop growing, developing, and improving our lives, the lives of our employees, our organization, and our community. Those who adopt a more positive outlook on life will achieve far more than those who are focused on the negative. When we are more positive, we tend to be more innovative, energetic, and resilient to all the trials that we face each day. Even more importantly, your positivism spreads to those around you, and your entire team becomes more innovative, energetic, and resilient. Remember to approach each situation that you face

- with no prejudice or preconceived ideas;
- with a learning attitude, being excited about new information;
- with positive expectancy;
- with a pen in hand taking notes;
- with a desire to hear not only what's being said, but also what it can trigger in your imagination; and
- with a "How can I use this?" attitude.

4. Help people laugh

I worked with a manager who started his monthly meetings with a joke. While it may not be the answer to every problem we ever face in our pressure-packed world, for some, it works. It helps people to relax, and if it forces them to laugh (even just a snicker—it doesn't have to be a great belly laugh, although that's better still) it's a healthy thing. It relaxes everyone and relieves stress, improves staff morale, increases productivity and decreases absenteeism. Have a good laugh and have fun. After all, the worst thing that can happen is that people may think you're a little nuts. Speaking of *NUTS*, in their nationwide bestseller about the zany antics at SouthWest Airlines, Kevin and Jackie Freiberg reveal the SouthWest way to a sense of humour. It's really quite simple, and has elements that we can all use in our own work environment, whatever that may be:

- Adopt a playful attitude. Go ahead and be silly, unconventional and find the humour in everyday work.
- Think funny. It doesn't mean we don't take business seriously. We just find the funny parts of that seriousness.
- Be the first to laugh.
- Laugh with, not at. Don't find humour at someone else's expense but it's sometimes ok to laugh with them to help ease their day.
- Be prepared to laugh at yourself. Or, as Ben Zander says, "Don't take yourself so damned seriously."
- Take yourself lightly but take your job and responsibilities seriously.(24)

5. Keep things in perspective

I have already shared my thoughts on work/life integration and balance. This issue is one that warrants repeating, and it's up to each of us, as managers and leaders, to remember what is important. Work occupies only a portion of our entire lives. When things are becoming difficult and stressful, it is important to keep it all in perspective. Is it really worth losing sleep over it? Is it worth affecting my health or my relations with staff, friends, or family? I shared the following story in *Common Sense Leadership* and will do so again now.

A professor stood before his philosophy class and had some items on display in front of him. There was an empty mayonnaise jar, a bag of golf balls, a box of pebbles, a box of sand, and two bottles of beer. When the class began, without speaking, he picked up the mayonnaise jar and proceeded to fill it with the golf balls. He then asked the students if the jar was full. They agreed that it was. The professor then picked up the box of pebbles and poured them into the jar. He shook the jar lightly, whereupon the pebbles gradually filled all the spaces between the golf balls. Once again, he asked the students if the jar was full and once again, they agreed that it was. He then picked up the box of sand and poured it into the jar. Of course, the sand filled all the remaining nooks and crannies and the students, once again, believed the jar to be full. (Don't worry, he didn't the pour the beer in.) The professor told the students that "this jar represents your life. The golf balls are the important things—your health, your family, your friend and your favourite passions—and if everything else was lost, your life would still be full. The pebbles are the other aspects of your life that are important but not critical, for example, your house, your car or your job. The sand is everything else—all the small stuff that tends to get in the way of what is really important. If you fill your life with all the small stuff first, there will be no room for what is truly important, represented by the golf balls and the pebbles. So, remember to pay attention to that which is truly important. The rest is just sand."

One of the students asked what the beer represented. The professor smiled and said, "I'm glad you asked. The beer just shows that no matter how full your life may seem, there's always room and time for a couple of beers with a friend."

Fun Things to Do at Work

Despite the desire to try and have fun at work, we can find ourselves at a loss as when deciding how to make our workplace fun yet productive. What is truly important is your attitude and approach. Try some of these ideas, or better yet, invite staff to come up with their own.

- Don't focus on the bad things that occur. Stuff happens. Forget about it and remember to celebrate the successes. Buy a cake. Bring some donuts in. Have fun.
- Do lunch occasionally. Get together with your colleagues. It doesn't need to be a liquid lunch like in "the good old days," but take an hour to decompress once in a while.
- The odd practical joke is fine, but don't get carried away.
- Halloween is a great time to dress up. Don't be afraid to look silly.
- Remember staff birthdays. Celebrate them in a fashion that the staff member appreciates. Not everyone wants a lot of pomp and ceremony, but most of us enjoy simply being remembered.
- Decorate work stations. Have a contest. Let the boss be the judge, or better yet, have several judges from other departments.
- Set up hockey pools.
- Sponsor contests that may connect with a corporate initiative, such as health and safety or even an accepted charity.
- Have a barbecue in the middle of the summer. The reason? There doesn't have to be one.
- Enjoy a pizza day once in a while.
- Exchange gifts at Christmas or contribute to a gift drive for those in the community who are less fortunate. You can have fun and do some good at the same time.
- Baby and wedding showers are always fan favourites (more for women than men, but I don't want to be accused of being sexist).
- Welcome new staff with coffee and donuts for everyone.
- Get the gang together outside work occasionally for a baseball day, a family skate day, or whatever else appeals to your group.
- Hold the occasional meeting outdoors in the good summer weather.

- Do anything else that helps keep the mood of the workplace relaxed and fun.

Can We Have Fun and Still Be a Leader?

The answer is an unequivocal yes.

According to a news report (source unknown), a certain private school in Brisbane was recently faced with a unique problem. A number of twelve-year-old girls were beginning to use lipstick and would put it on in the bathroom. That was fine, but after they put on their lipstick they would press their lips to the mirror, leaving dozens of little lip prints.

Every night the maintenance man would remove them and the next day the girls would put them back.

Finally, the principal decided that something had to be done. She called all the girls to the bathroom and met them there with the maintenance man. She explained that all these lip prints were causing a major problem for the custodian, who had to clean the mirrors every night (you can imagine the yawns from the little princesses). To demonstrate how difficult it had been to clean the mirrors, she asked the maintenance man to show the girls how much effort was required.

He took out a long-handled squeegee, dipped it in the toilet, and cleaned the mirror with it. Since then, there have been no lip prints on the mirrors.

The principal was clearly a leader who understood how important her role as an educator was. In addition, I'll bet they had many a good laugh about the incident afterward.

Have fun.

> ### *Key Messages*
> ### *Let's Have Fun*
>
> For most of us, if you remember when you were a kid, you'll remember how easy it was to laugh so happily at so many things. It remains my opinion that work should be as natural as play, so let's learn to have fun while we're there.
>
> 1. If you're not having fun at work, it's time for a change.
> 2. If there is a fun environment, it can lead to good business results, such as reduced absenteeism, engaged staff, and less turnover.
> 3. Adopt a playful but professional attitude about work. It's okay to think and be silly. But that doesn't mean that we don't take business seriously.

Chapter 7:

Be Nice

A little bit of fragrance always clings to the hand that gives you roses.
—Chinese proverb

In the *Toronto Star*, on July 30, 2011, a front-page story was titled "They're Actually Just Being Nice. Seriously." The issue being referenced was "an advertising campaign sweeping through Canada's largest cities, encouraging people to be good, do good, and encourage goodness everywhere." One of the principles I focused on in *Common Sense Leadership*, and one that I have continuously promoted in subsequent teachings and presentations, is the importance, as a manager and a leader, of being nice to the people that you meet each day.

I originally struggled with using the words "be nice" because it just didn't sound particularly profound or remotely intellectual, but no matter how I wrestled with this issue, in the end, encouraging all of us to simply be nice to each other was the key message. It was also something that my parents, who both lived through the Great Depression and World War II, tried diligently to foster within me and my five siblings.

When I speak about "being nice" to others, I envision a world where we all smile a lot, where we say "good morning" and "good night" to our staff, and maybe even to strangers, and where we are all polite and use good manners with everyone we come into contact with. This really should apply at home, in the community, and at work.

However, for the purposes of this discussion, my concern is primarily the workplace. Being nice to all people at work may not guarantee fame, fortune, or organizational success, but it will most assuredly do no harm. Be nice to others. It is an important step to building positive, effective relationships. This doesn't mean that we should focus only on a network of colleagues, superiors, or any others who can help advance us in our careers. Perpetually being nice to them while at the same time being a jerk with your own staff or others in the organization who may not appear to carry as much influence as you may believe may mark you as disingenuous.

For my part, over my entire career in leadership and management roles, I have worked hard to build positive relations with all staff, managers, bosses, councillors, board members, and union representatives. Does that mean that I always suck up to those in positions of influence and disregard everyone else? Does it suggest that I won't make the tough decisions or that I have difficulty with saying no to various requests? It doesn't mean any of that, nor does it mean that I change with the wind.

No way. It means being pleasant and decent with everyone I come into contact with. I have discovered that the organizational leaders who are the most successful and respected by their staff are those who are routinely nice to everybody. They are also—and this is an important lesson—the ones who get to know their staff as individuals. They realize that their staff have their own unique lives and that—as I repeatedly remind folks—everyone we meet is fighting a battle of some kind.

When staff are having difficult days, it is best to remember that the cause of their difficulty may have nothing to do with the workplace but rather may be the result of one of the battles they are fighting away from work. None of this implies that in building relationships with your staff you must become best friends with any of them. Just understand them. They are not merely human resources. As one person told me, "It's face time that counts." Don't hide in the office. Get out there and know people. Know what they do and be nice.

From many municipal colleagues over the years, I have been asked what the secret is to building good relations with councillors. There is no magic. Remember that they are ordinary people who simply represent other people in the community. They also have issues, challenges, goals, promises to keep, principles, and philosophies.

I haven't always agreed with municipal councillors, but I have always tried to be pleasant, and I have enjoyed some success. Relationships with them are no different than with any other person. There are no guarantees. In all relationships and in all dealings with people generally, there is no perfect world. As a result, some people we meet are simply jerks. It's useful to remember that at times we can all be jerks, but hopefully only temporarily, as we are influenced by battles we are facing elsewhere.

Regardless of my best intentions and my desire to be nice, some folks appear determined to be nasty no matter what the rest of us do. These are, as Robert Sutton calls them, "certified assholes." In his bestseller *The No Asshole Rule,* Sutton shares what he calls The Dirty Dozen, everyday actions that assholes use (his words, not mine). They are complete opposites of actions that nice people take. How would you see yourself? The assholes engage in

- Personal insults
- Invading one's "personal territory"

- Uninvited physical contact
- Threats and intimidation, both verbal and nonverbal
- "Sarcastic jokes" and "teasing" used as insult delivery systems
- Withering e-mail flames
- Status slaps intended to humiliate their victims
- Public shaming or "status degradation" rituals
- Rude interruptions
- Two-faced attacks
- Dirty looks
- Treating people as if they are invisible(25)

It is because of these types of behaviour that many organizations are now implementing zero-tolerance policies. This stuff leads to a toxic environment, low employee morale, loss of trust, increased stress and anxiety, reduced productivity, increased turnover, and a generally negative environment for all. Here are four things that each of us can do in response to these acts:

- When you witness any of these actions, firmly but politely ask the person to stop. Make sure they understand that you don't appreciate it, and neither do your colleagues.
- Don't listen to this type of thing. Walk away if you can. Delete the e-mails. Certainly don't join in.
- Don't contribute to the areas of the workplace where this is particularly prevalent. Try to make those areas more positive if you can. For example, if you know that "the guys" gather out on the loading dock to engage in this activity, clean up the loading dock so it's not as conducive as they might like. If the lunchroom is another centre of activity, either avoid it or help clean it up. Make it uncomfortable for the perpetrators.
- As a manager, make sure policies are in place that forbid this type of conduct. When you know it is happening, deal quickly and effectively to stop it.

- For staff, if there are no policies, speak up. Ask—in fact, demand—that they be put in place. Don't ignore it, hoping that it will go away. It won't.

For all of us, it is important to remember that, regardless of the role, position, or status of any individual we deal with at work, at home, or in the community, we all need to be kind, decent, and respectful of others. There are a number of ways that we can ensure that we all do our part to be kind and decent. The following are some common-sense behaviours that we can all easily engage in that will allow everybody to enjoy their work far more. Let's start with a principle that we have all heard from our parents, captured in one form or another by all the world's religions. From my own upbringing, it is simply called the Golden Rule.

The Golden Rule

"Do unto others as you would have them do unto you." It's really quite simple. If you want others to treat you nicely and with courtesy, you should do likewise. If you want others to be pleasant every day, then you should show them the same degree of pleasantness with the same degree of regularity. We have all met and worked with someone in our lives who just was not that nice. I don't understand it, because the principle is so simple.

Don't be nasty. It does not pay any dividends whatsoever. You can be the hardest-working person on the team. You can put in the longest hours. You can have an IQ that's off the charts. However, it is all for naught if you don't treat others well. Starting now, make it a personal habit to treat everyone that you come into contact with nicely. Try for a "no exceptions" policy in this regard. You will be amazed at the results.

The Resolution Centre, an organization dedicated to workplace conflict prevention and resolution, has created a list of behaviours intended to demonstrate and promote greater respect in the workplace. Distribute these throughout the workplace and, more importantly, practise them and expect others to do likewise. In other words, "Do unto others as you would have them do unto you."

1. Always treat people with courtesy, politeness, kindness, and ultimately, how you would like to be treated.
2. Listen to what others have to say before expressing your viewpoint.
3. Never butt in or talk over another person.
4. Encourage others to express their opinions and ideas.
5. Improve your work by using others' ideas and credit them for their ideas.
6. Never put people down, disparage them, call them names, or insult them.
7. Do not belittle, criticize little things, demean, or patronize others. A series of small comments over time can amount to bullying.
8. If you would prefer not to do a task, chances are, neither would your co-worker. Share the load.
9. Regardless of race, religion, gender, age, or other orientation, always treat people equally.
10. Ensure that your workplace maintains an equal opportunity policy and that you are familiar with it.
11. Ensure that praise, recognition, and appreciation is abundant in your workplace.

Good Manners

When you follow the Golden Rule, good manners naturally follow. They are a learned behaviour that too many people seem to forget. When I was young, if I failed to show proper manners, I would be on the receiving end of a good smack. It was a different world in those days, but the importance of good manners are as valid today in life and in business just as they were when I was young.

Good manners should be nothing more than common courtesy. However, all too often it seems like more of a lost art. The manners that most of us were taught in our youth still need to apply as the years accumulate, regardless of whether we are at home, at work, or in the community. This isn't rocket science. These include the following courtesies:

- Don't talk with your mouth full.
- Keep your elbows off the table.
- Say please and thank you.
- Hold the door for others.
- Respect your elders.
- Don't interrupt.
- Listen.
- Share with others.
- Take turns.
- If you don't have anything nice to say about someone, don't say anything at all.

None of us is so important that these rules somehow no longer apply to us. We sometimes excuse rude behaviour by saying we were just preoccupied with our own thoughts or troubles and our own feelings of self-importance. It is immaterial what position we hold in the organization. We must still say please and thank you to our staff, our colleagues, or simply the nice person who serves us coffee at the donut shop. It is really quite easy. Even more impressive is when we take the time to pass along a hand-written note of thanks or appreciation to a staff member or colleague. It's amazing how far such a simple gesture will go in building support for you as a leader and as a kind and decent person. Poor manners are inexcusable in any business, any culture, and any relationship.

Say Good Morning and Good Night

A specific example of good manners is greeting our colleagues with "good morning" or saying "good night" when we leave. Many years ago, entertainer George Burns would close out his radio show with the words "Good night, Gracie," an expression of love to his wife, Gracie. What a nice way to end the show. We should all take more time to extend these common courtesies.

It never ceases to amaze me that there are so many people in our world who have so much difficulty simply and sincerely sharing a "good morning," "hello," "hi," "good night," or "how ya doin'" with people they meet each day. For some, I would be happy to see a smile or nod of acknowledgment from them. My goodness, there are so many who can pass one another in a stairwell or in a hallway when you are the only ones present, and yet they still manage to not look each other in the eye, smile, nod, or just say hello.

Let's bring this back to our own leadership. We need to expect this of ourselves, for if we fail to do so, how can we expect our staff to be pleasant with each other, with our customers, and with our colleagues? Try it. It doesn't hurt. Smile. Offer these simple greetings to everyone you pass.

As a manager and a leader, you are not above this common courtesy, so don't ever fall into the trap of believing that you are too important to acknowledge your staff or colleagues. I don't remember the names or faces of everyone I meet, but frankly, what does it matter? I still do my best to smile and greet them properly. We don't need to wait for HR to create an official policy or value encouraging all staff to be nice to each other. Do it because it's the right thing to do. As someone once told me, "Smiles are free, so give them freely."

Gossip—Don't Do It

Another lesson from my parents, one that has a powerful impact on workplace culture, is "If you have nothing nice to say about somebody, say nothing." It is as true today as it was 50 years ago. There is nothing so harmful or destructive to a person than to be the target of gossip and rumour. In this regard, I am referring to unproven "facts" about others, or hearsay. This often involves personal, confidential information that can be destructive and hurtful.

To encourage or even allow gossip in your department is likely to contribute to the following concerns in the work environment:

- The overall atmosphere becomes toxic, as gossip never stops at one person or one situation.
- It leads to high anxiety, low morale, and loss of trust among staff.
- Productivity is adversely affected.
- Absenteeism increases.
- Staff become divided as they take sides on issues.
- Feelings are hurt and reputations tarnished.
- Gossipers may hurt their own chances for promotion.
- Turnover increases.
- Complaints increase; grievances and/or charges of harassment or bullying are filed.
- In the worst cases, violence in the workplace results.

Don't listen to it, don't engage in it, and certainly don't pass it along when you do hear it—and we all hear it, every day. Always speak highly of your friends, family, colleagues, associates, staff, and bosses, and they in turn are more likely to speak highly of you. In fact, it has been suggested to me that people who hear secondhand that you have said something nice about them are inclined to have very positive reactions to the news. However, when they hear bad things said about them secondhand, the impact can be more devastating than when they hear the same views directly. In my training sessions, I always try to finish with, "If you did not like today's session, please tell me. If you thought it was great, tell everybody else." Bad news or comments that are less than positive should be passed directly to those involved. Gossip and rumours are great fodder for soap operas, but they have no value otherwise. As a manager, you need to set a good example for your staff, always remain positive, and make a sincere effort to look for the very best in every situation and in every person. The results will always include a less stressful, more open, and more honest work environment, with positive working relationships, increased cooperation, fewer conflicts, and greater productivity.

Community Work

As organizations and as individuals, we exist in a larger community setting. We cannot operate our business in isolation of everybody else. As individuals, we cannot continue to take from the community, expecting that the simple act of paying our taxes is the only obligation that we have to the greater good of the community. Improving community relations effectively serves the workplace as workers feel more engaged in their community and more like they are making a difference. They are not just creating a product or a service; they are part of a larger initiative that has potential benefit for the entire community. There is always an element of pride associated with giving something back.

Increasingly, corporations are being expected to operate in an environment where the public can be assured of safe products and practices. Consider these experiences:

- Johnson and Johnson and the Tylenol scare a number of years ago
- Nike's response to charges of abusive labour practices in their factories abroad
- Lead found in toys manufactured in China recently
- Shell Oil sinking the Brent Spar in the North Sea
- The BP oil spill in the Gulf of Mexico
- Molson Breweries' campaigns to curb drunk driving
- Ronald McDonald Houses sited near numerous children's hospitals

In each of these cases and hundreds of others, the public is demanding greater accountability on the part of the organizations and their leaders. We want (and, in fact, demand) assurances that they operate in safe environments, that we promote the proper and respectful use of limited natural resources, that we are not contaminating the environment, that we reduce waste, and that we maintain ethical business practices.

However, these responsibilities are not limited to organizational leaders. Rather, they extend to all of us. We all have an obligation to give back to our communities in more ways than by simply paying our taxes. We can all show leadership by giving more to charity, by helping run organizations for underprivileged kids, coaching a soccer or hockey team, being a Boy Scout or Girl Guide leader, sitting on boards and commissions, volunteering at the local soup kitchen, helping the homeless, or doing countless other things to give back. It may take a little extra time or money, but if we have it to give, everyone benefits. This is one way each and every one of us can demonstrate true leadership qualities.

Don't Accept Diversity—Promote It!

Regardless of the challenges that both the United States and Canada have faced in their past (North versus South, French versus English, gay rights, religious differences, etc.) the current makeup of both countries, and most of the Western world, is one of acceptance of every culture, background, nationality, and orientation imaginable.

In most organizations, especially with the recent elimination of mandatory retirement in most jurisdictions, we have as many as four distinct generations in our workforce. Every person brings value to our lives and our workplaces, regardless of their age, sex, sexual orientation, race, colour, creed, or religion. We are all just people. Don't judge others on any factor other than the value they bring to their communities and their organizations, and we all bring some value.

In some cases, we tend to think that by tearing others down, we may increase our own feelings of self-worth and self-esteem. Perhaps worse, we pass judgment based purely on first impressions, such as their taste in clothes, tattoos, body piercings, excess weight, a lisp, their haircut, and so on. Wait until you know them before you pass judgment on them. Avoid taking a "holier than thou," attitude as you may find you really aren't any better (or any worse) than those you have so quickly and easily passed judgment on.

Don't Be Angry

Once upon a time, I may have thought that there was some value to getting angry on occasion (generally I am considered "laid back," but not 100 percent of the time), as though it would somehow demonstrate my leadership to others. Nothing could be further from the truth. All that it really demonstrates is that one is losing control and it will lead only to a loss of self-esteem, respect, appreciation, and ultimately, the potential deterioration of what might have been a very positive relationship.

I can assure you that after a career spanning close to 40 years in management/leadership roles, I have yet to make one good decision or take one positive action when I was angry. As Sutton notes in *The No Asshole Rule* about one case referred to him,

> Ethan qualifies as a certified asshole: his temper is legendary; he treats his co-workers as rivals, routinely insulting and belittling them; his nasty late-night e-mail rants are infamous; and, not surprisingly, many insiders refuse to work with him ... Meanwhile, HR managers and, at times, senior executives were spending huge chunks of time running interference between Ethan and the company's support network. In the prior five years, several colleagues and administrative assistants had lodged "hostile workplace" complaints against Ethan. The

company also spent a substantial amount of money on Ethan's anger management classes and counselling.(26)

In this instance, the company calculated the cost of Ethan's bad behaviour to be approximately $160,000 for one year only. What might it be costing your organization?

If you feel yourself getting angry in any situation, walk away, cool down, calm down, and go to plan B. It will help dramatically if you recognize the signs that you are losing your cool and getting angry and you can most assuredly count on losing control and respect when you do get angry. Besides, like the schoolyard bully, eventually, as my parents would say, "The bully will get his comeuppance too. There will always be someone who is bigger and stronger than him." Don't get angry and don't try to bully others. It just doesn't work.

Recognizing and Appreciating Others

Good managers and outstanding leaders always take time to recognize and appreciate others. In turn, that recognition and appreciation result in a positive impact on our workplace culture. Generally, when we think of reward and recognition programs, most of us think of the official programs created by organizations that recognize staff once they have survived a certain number of years with the organization. It always reminds me of the bumper stickers in the United States that proclaim "I survived I-95" (or some such thing).

While I support organizational programs that recognize staff for having achieved certain milestone anniversaries with the organization, I don't think it's such a grand thing if it serves only to measure some degree of endurance by the employees. I want the employees to see these milestones as something truly memorable. Making their time memorable is something that is unique to each organization, but certainly a good place to start is for each employee to feel that they have been truly appreciated during their time with the employer.

Because each organization and its culture is as individual as each of us, there is no prescribed pattern to follow. We have to understand our staff as individuals and how they fit with each other and with the organization as a whole. Only then is the recognition a good thing.

The approach taken by General Motors may be dramatically different from the one taken by a small municipality, which is also different from that adopted by a large teaching hospital. In addition to these milestones, many organizations reward employees for achieving something in the line of duty that can be seen to go above and beyond. For instance, perhaps they have invented something particularly exciting or positive or have taken a leadership role in the company that is well outside their normal duties or expectations of the job. These are good things and worthy of recognition.

However, outside these milestones or outstanding accomplishments is the day-to-day recognition that is so easy and yet so often forgotten by so managers. It is this recognition program that goes to the notion of being nice.

As leaders and managers, it is incumbent upon each of us to foster a culture of recognition. This cannot be imposed on us by edict or the proclamation of an HR policy. Also we may not be able to turn around the rest of the company or the community by ourselves, but that is not what is important. However, we want to ensure that we show appreciation for our own staff and contribute positively to our own spheres of influence.

We can start by making sure we smile at work. We see our glass as half full. We see every staff member as an individual, each with his or her own battles to fight. We connect with them as individuals. We say "thank you" to each person we meet each day. We recognize them when they do a job particularly well.

In some cases, the appreciation may go beyond simple thanks, to gift cards or movie passes for special achievements. There is no single way to appreciate or recognize staff. Be creative and be considerate. However, be sincere and don't overdo it. I once had a boss who was one of the finest gentlemen I have ever had the pleasure of knowing. He thanked me for everything I did. I have, on many occasions since, told people that I believe I could have committed manslaughter and he would have thanked me for doing it well. There are limits. Thanks are important, and recognition for outstanding work or effort is critical, but it must be sincere and it must be appropriate in terms of degree and timing.

You should also take care to give out recognition at the appropriate time and place. Sometimes, and for some people, it may be best to give it in front of colleagues. For others, recognition is best given in private. Again, knowing each staff member as an individual will ensure that you make the right choice. Hopefully, whatever approach you take to recognition, it generates interest and enthusiasm among all staff.

One final note: reward and recognition is not something that falls within the exclusive purview of management. It is something all staff can engage in. It is easy, it is inexpensive, it builds team spirit, and it contributes meaningfully to the enjoyment of everyone's job. It needs to be seen to be part of the organizational culture. Best of all, it allows everybody the opportunity to just "be nice."

Key Messages
Don't Forget to Be Nice

Part of being nice is having good manners. Remember, the good manners you learned at home carry over to your everyday life, both personal and at work.

1. Relationships are of critical importance, and relationships start and end with being nice, kind, and respectful toward others.
2. Don't forget to say "good morning" and "good night" to as many staff as you can.
3. Don't be angry. No good decisions or actions ever come about when we are angry.
4. Remember to recognize your staff on a day-to-day basis for all the good things that they do and the great things they accomplish. It only takes a moment to say "thanks."

Chapter 8:

The Importance of Ethics and Integrity

Dare to be yourself in the face of adversity. Choosing right over wrong, ethics over convenience ... these are the choices that measure your life. Travel the path of integrity ... for there is never the wrong time to do the right thing.

—Anon

Let me start by noting that the words *ethics* and *integrity* are used interchangeable by most folks. The distinction, in my mind, is that *ethics* refers to behavioural matters while *integrity* addresses consistency of behaviour.

I define *ethics*, for my own purposes and for the purposes of this book (as well as numerous presentations) as doing the right thing at the right time for the right reason. *Integrity*, as a result, is making sure that every action we take applies that definition consistently. There can be no exceptions.

If we intended to effect improvements in the workplace, having fun and being nice with others are important practices, but they will ultimately be meaningless unless we are ethical and act 100 percent of the time with absolute integrity.

We cannot allow ourselves to slip into a mode where we justify unethical behaviour by saying, "It's okay, because he deserved it anyway," or that "It's no big deal—everybody else does it." It really is a simple practice to get into, and yet we hear of major transgressions every day by all manner of people who should know better. Our parents taught us that it is not right to steal from others, and not one of the major religions condones theft, but it happens daily. The "bad guys" are not the only ones doing it; kids are caught shoplifting, staff are caught stealing from their employers, fraud and tax evasion (just nicer ways of saying "theft") account for huge corporate financial losses every year.

We need only to consider the cases of Conrad Black or Garth Drabinsky. All too often, teachers or kids' coaches engage in inappropriate conduct, sexual or otherwise, while athletes are still frequently caught using performance enhancing drugs. (A quick word of clarification is needed here. The vast majority of teachers and coaches are honest, hardworking, ethical people who unfortunately and far too easily get tarred with the same brush as those whose intentions are less pure. The same can be said about athletes. It is a minority who try to gain an unfair advantage over the competition by using illicit drugs. To all the rest, my apologies are extended.)

Let us not forget the politicians who abuse their power and position to conduct themselves unethically. Consider, if you will, the cases of Rod Blagojevich, the Bellamy and Gomery inquiries in Canada, President Clinton's indiscretions and attempted cover-up with Monica Lewinsky, President Nixon's impeachment, or a Canadian senator's recent flirtatious e-mails with a Chinese news correspondent. Pick up any daily newspaper and you will find them to be full of examples of unethical conduct every day of the week. Ethics, for many, is like the weather—we like to talk about it, but too often we seem powerless to do much to change it, for regardless how much time we spend discussing it, there are still too many who just don't get it.

Another aspect of ethics, one that does not receive enough attention, is the issue of trust. Suffice it to say that when we hire our staff, or even when they look to their managers and leaders, there is a perpetual expectation that each of us will do the right thing for the right reason at the right time. We must trust staff to do right and they, in turn, should expect that we will do likewise.

One of my favourite pet peeves in the workplace is micromanagement. Those who micromanage simply don't trust their staff to do what they have been trained to do. Staff are usually in the position to know what is best under any given circumstance. If they are unsure, their manager should serve as leader and coach with advice, counsel, and guidance. However, if it takes two of us to do one job (manager and employee) then, frankly, one of us is not needed. If we can't trust staff and ultimately micromanage them, this leads to duplication of effort, a loss of morale, and gross inefficiency. Throughout this chapter, I will make reference to the issue of trust and its implications for the workplace.

For now, managers should contemplate: What does it mean to act ethically and with integrity ever day? Forget the politicians, the athletes, and all the others that occupy prime space in the daily news as we hear about their behavioural inconsistencies, their bribes, their sexual exploits, or abuses of drugs and alcohol. I am more concerned about two broad areas of ethics that we need to address.

The first area is *managerial mischief*, including illegal, unethical, or questionable practices on the part of individual managers or organizations. These behaviours are most often intentional and typically cause serious legal, financial, or reputational harm. Stealing supplies, products, or money from the company is an obvious example of managerial mischief. Engaging in fraudulent conduct is another. Other examples include employing child labour, engaging in illegal labour practices, damaging or polluting the environment, and knowingly selling unsafe products. There has been a great deal written about managerial mischief, which has led many to believe that ethics is merely a matter of preaching the basics of what is right and wrong. In these instances, we all know what is right and what is wrong. More often, though, ethics is a matter of dealing with dilemmas where it is not clear what is right or wrong, otherwise known as moral mazes.

Moral mazes falls into that broad area of ethics that includes the numerous ethical problems that managers must deal with every day, such as potential conflicts of interest, inappropriate use of resources, and mismanagement of contracts and agreements. In short, all managers/ leaders should be expected to conduct themselves in a manner that is simply legally and ethically correct. However, many of their decisions do not fall into neat black-and-white scenarios but rather shades of gray. This is the area that I have had to deal with most in my career. Managers are often simply not sure of the ground they stand on when it comes to the ethicality of certain actions or behaviours. It is usually this gray area that causes the most stress, and managers and leaders have to be particularly vigilant in fostering a culture of openness so that people will feel comfortable coming to management and asking about these dilemmas before they act in a way that causes a breach of ethics.

One of the problems with implementing a system of organizational ethics is that we all like to believe we are ethical. However, how many of us cheat on our taxes? Take office supplies for personal use? Enjoy unauthorized extended lunches? Perform personal chores on company time? It is not as easy as one might first expect. Any one incident may go undetected or may appear to be minor in nature. However, if we become careless or are not sufficiently vigilant, those minor issues can grow out of control.

If a manager has a contract that has approved the purchase of ten computers for $20,000, and that manager is able to get eleven computers for $20,500, most would turn a blind eye to that indiscretion. But for the City of Toronto, that sort of carelessness became a major problem.

The City of Toronto—The Bellamy Inquiry

Beginning in 2002, the Honourable Madame Justice Denise E. Bellamy conducted two inquiries dealing with questionable business/political practices at the City of Toronto. The incident that triggered this massive investigation revolved around an approved computer leasing plan that grew from a relatively small obligation of $14 million to more than $83 million without corresponding council approvals. In fact, the essence of the problem was that the leasing company essentially bought the extended contract by wining and dining staff and politicians. The staff failed to take adequate precautions to ensure proper protocols were followed, and politicians basked in the pleasures of life that the salespeople were casting their way. The inquiry lasted three and a half years, encompassing 214 days of public hearings, 124,000 pages of documentation, 156 witnesses, 22 parties with official standing, and more than 60 lawyers. The problems that were unveiled throughout the hearings are perhaps best explained by Madame Justice Bellamy herself, who, on pages 5 and 6 of her executive summary, notes,

> As the stories in this report will make very clear, people made mistakes. Some people disgraced themselves, failed in their duty to their City, lied, put self-interest first, or simply did not do their jobs. Many City processes and procedures were not up to the high standards that the people of the City of Toronto have a right to expect. Some people did not show the leadership expected of them. Lines of responsibility and accountability were unclear or nonexistent. There was poor communication between people who should have been talking to one another and excessive communication between people who should have stayed at arms' length.

The executive summary covered some 108 pages. The full report is a mammoth document, but suffice it to say, 241 recommendations were made that provided the Council and staff of the City of Toronto with guidance regarding Codes of Conduct, hiring practices, training of staff and councillors, staff and council relations, conflicts of interest, complaints, investigations, lobbying activities, and the hiring of a full-time integrity commissioner. These inquiries cost the taxpayers of Toronto millions of dollars. However, hopefully, the lessons learned will continue to be of significant benefit to all levels of government in both Canada and the United States.

The learnings from the Bellamy Inquiry can apply to all organizations and to each of us as individuals. Not all people who become tainted by this sort of scandal set out to intentionally put self-interest first or to engage in any illegal or unethical conduct. However, if we are not alert to the possibilities or fail to be vigilant about our conduct, or even public perceptions of that conduct, the result will not be a healthy one.

Personal Ethics

Ultimately, we can only ever be responsible for our own actions and our own decisions. While we should rightly be guided by the organizational culture, values, practices, codes, and programs, we must also be guided by the same "golden rule" that has been referred to as well as our own personal values. Any organizational culture starts with individuals, so it is valuable to look at developing principles and values at the individual level first.

Michael Josephson, in *The Six Pillars of Character*, identified six core values and principles that should be an integral part of a personal code of ethics and should be a critical part of our organizational culture and value system:

1. **Trustworthiness** includes qualities such as integrity, honesty, reliability, and loyalty. It can also include being consistent in our

decision making and being true to established organizational values, principles, and practices. We avoid bad-faith excuses or unwise and unclear commitments. Unlike when we were in high school, we cannot claim, "The dog ate my homework." It is critical, if we want a reputation of being trustworthy, that our behaviour always reflect truthfulness, sincerity, and candour. While it is important that we trust others in our relationships, at work and elsewhere, it is even more critical that others can trust us.

2. **Respect** includes respect for both ourselves as well as others. It also encompasses the need to respect all people regardless of race, creed, colour, age, or other distinguishing features. We cannot allow ourselves to engage in intimidation or coercion of others, always promoting autonomy and individuality. In the workplace, this allows us to establish and maintain an environment free from any act of harassment, discrimination, or unfair treatment. We must, at all times, be cognizant of the damage to our staff and their overall productivity that can result from any invasion of personal privacy, gossip and rumours, offensive language, lack of workplace cleanliness, and inappropriate noise.

3. **Responsibility** means we are always accountable for our actions and decisions. We are also responsible to ensure that we pursue excellence in all that we do. We lead by example. We must be reliable, exercise self-control, and be perpetually focused on improving ourselves and increasing our value to others and to the workplace. Ultimately, we cannot be responsible for the actions and behaviours of others. However, we are always responsible for our own behaviour and conduct. Make sure that we do the right thing at the right time for the right reason.

4. **Fairness** and transparency are always demonstrated in terms of settling disputes or dividing/assigning resources; we must not show favouritism or prejudice and must quickly and effectively, correcting mistakes or injustices affecting others when we have

the power to do so. As will be noted in the chapter on conflict management, if we ignore them, problems that we have in the workplace will not simply go away. They will continue to fester and in most cases will only get worse. As a manager, it is up to each of us to deal with disputes fairly and effectively.

5. **Caring** and being genuinely concerned for the welfare of others includes being generous with our time, our energy, and our money. Always remember to be kinder than necessary, because every person we meet on any day may be facing some kind of personal battle and that person badly needs our support and our understanding. We should, when reflecting on our daily successes or failures, be able to revel in the number of times that we are able, every day, to help make somebody else's day and life just a little bit better. It may be done by helping an employee with a problem (personal or professional), letting someone in line in front of us, giving a homeless person a cup of coffee, or just holding the door for someone who is struggling with his or her groceries. Caring and compassion are not lost art forms, as some seem to believe. They just need each of us to enact them more often.

6. **Citizenship** prescribes how we behave as part of a larger community of people. We must know and obey the laws of the land, whether the challenges be faced while at work or while at home. We must be aware of the issues of the day, be concerned about our environment, and volunteer our time and energy. We must all be prepared to do our part to make our world a better place in which we work and play.

Organizational Ethics Programs

Just as each individual addresses his or her own ethics, organizations must should have policies in place to support collective ethical behaviour. For every organization, it is imperative that programs be established that achieve the following:

- Discourage conduct by staff that is illegal, may incur a reputational liability, may harm the organization in any way, or may violate any relevant policies
- Ensure compliance with all legal and regulatory requirements as well as organizational policies and standards
- Encourage a culture of ethical conduct and the promotion of an acceptance of questioning or challenging, as appropriate, decisions seen to be inconsistent with that culture
- Deliver appropriate education to the entire organization
- Address the managerial mischief and moral mazes referred to by Carter McNamara

While we can collectively and corporately promote the "golden rule" (and that is something that we should continue to strive to achieve), our efforts are subjected to constant undermining, especially for those in positions of power. Pressure is applied by vendors, developers, friends, family, neighbours, political constituents, and others, all seeking business opportunities, jobs, concessions, deals, or favours. Any of us may be subjected to temptation through drinks, food, rounds of golf, and gifts.

In some instances, the temptations are not particularly overt but instead may be much more insidious. I can remember, in one case, having just received organizational approval for a new ethics program, one that would give staff and managers clear guidelines as to what was considered appropriate behaviour and what was not appropriate.

The very next day, I was contacted by a consulting firm that I regularly did business with and one that I would continue to do business with for years to come. Therefore, their approach to me this day was not intended to curry any favour with me. They considered it to be a legitimate business decision. Their new owners were inviting a number of key clients to their private box at the Rogers Centre in Toronto to watch the Toronto Blue Jays game—all expenses paid. I was one of the invitees. My first reaction, one that is really quite natural, was to be thrilled at the prospect of watching a game from a private box. What a treat. However, sober second thought took over and I found myself obliged to decline their very kind offer. It would have been considered quite inappropriate, especially in a public sector arena.

Organizational managers must adhere to established ethics programs and must promote a daily ethical culture. They must be seen to walk the talk. They can demonstrate ethical leadership by being open, honest, transparent, fair and trustworthy to all, regardless of their position, occupation, or standing or status in the community. They must present a perpetual ethical role model for their staff and others.

What Does an Ethical Workplace Look Like?

In light of these considerations, what most workplaces need is a single, comprehensive (but simple) ethics policy/program, a well-thought-out slate of values that all staff know, support, and understand as well as a leadership team that is prepared to walk the talk and is obsessed with fairness.

I sincerely believe that we all know the differences between right and wrong, at least in most instances. With this in mind, why would I suggest we go to the trouble of creating ethics programs at work? Simply put, there are situations we face in life and, for the purposes of this book, at work, that are not black and white but rather come in shades of grey. The result is that most of us find such guidelines helpful when facing situations where the answer may not be as clear as we would like.

Many workplaces have policies that deal with a code of conduct, harassment and discrimination, behavioural expectations, conflict resolution, conflict of interest, confidentiality, plus other assorted and related but unconnected policies that often serve to confuse rather than enlighten staff. These policies are intended to prevent cases of "managerial mischief" referred to previously. Purchasing policies, hiring practices, and risk management programs are all examples of policies and practices intended to guide staff to ensure that their behaviour and conduct is as honourable and morally correct as possible.

Most often, the organization's ethics program is not called such and is nothing more than a collection of well-intended initiatives that address unique issues and problems as they arise or as they are raised in various forums. These policies and practices, as accumulated over time, should be cast aside to make room for one comprehensive ethics program that includes, not only a core policy but also behavioural expectations for *all* staff, communication strategies, educational programs, and a process for the filing, investigating, and adjudication of complaints. Hotlines, helplines, and mechanisms to discuss difficult challenges must all be part of the overall package. The program cannot be seen as a one-time initiative.

The management of ethics must be seen to be an ongoing concern, subject to regular audit, review, consideration, and renewal. The spirit and intent is to promote preferred behaviour and to be proactive in facing and resolving potential problems. It needs to become engrained as part of the very fabric of the organization as a key management practice. It cannot be just "one of those HR things" that staff talk about while rolling their eyes.

Again, each organization is unique. As a result, a cookie-cutter policy is unlikely to inspire anyone. A better approach would be to create a code of conduct that speaks to the importance of ethical practices such as treating one another with respect, being service oriented, acting in the best interests of the organization, at all times being professional, not accepting gifts or bribes, avoiding conflicts of interest, keeping confidential information confidential, and upholding the spirit and intent of all applicable laws. Contact colleagues in the field to see what others have or are doing. You don't need to reinvent the wheel, but it is a wise practice to learn from others. Another example of a code of conduct, from General Electric, can be found later in this chapter.

Values

A healthy organization and a healthy culture have values that are important guiding lights for all staff to see and believe in. We have all seen statements such as "we demonstrate integrity in everything we do." Another is "every employee of ABC will provide excellence in service through collaboration, partnerships and teamwork in an atmosphere of trust and respect." Still others try to assure that "we will provide an accessible, inclusive environment which values the diversity of our staff and the community."

They are all nice words, but do they actually inspire the staff to greater heights or higher levels of performance? Not necessarily. More important is that the leadership walks the talk and maintains a focus on those values at all times.

While the methods I learned when I was young often seemed harsh, the point remains that my own parents practised what they preached. They walked the talk, for if they didn't, it would have been impossible to truly teach and coach me on the types of proper and acceptable conduct. This was also the clear message conveyed to me by many of those that I interviewed for my first book. There can be nothing more deflating than to hear organizational leaders talk about ethics, fairness, and respect yet conduct themselves in a totally different fashion. We cannot have one set of rules for staff and something different for the leadership. "Do as I say, not as I do" simply does not cut it in a contemporary workplace.

Leadership decisions and actions must reflect organizational values; in fact, leaders would be well advised to regularly remind themselves and others of the existence, content, spirit, and intent of their ethics program. One way to remind staff is to include a discussion, as part of every performance review, on how each employee has demonstrated adherence to the organizational values in their behaviour and conduct over the last year. If nothing else, it at least forces some discussion of ethics and values generally. That sort of reminder will keep ethics and values front and centre with all staff.

In addition, most reasonably progressive workplaces will post a set of core values somewhere on their walls for all to see. In most instances, there is some type of accompanying statement that says "everybody who works here believes in these values supports them and lives life by them" (or some such thing). Sadly, the reality is more likely to be that the senior leadership team, with or without their board, creates the values, with or without the help of an outside consultant. Hopefully, those core values then reflect the behaviours of all members of the organization. They spend a day or two at a retreat and come up with some words or phrases that are bound to impress anybody who happens to read them. However, they become meaningful only if every staff member knows what they are all about, supports them, and indeed allows them to guide their workplace behaviour.

Every employer should have four or five key values that become integrated into every business activity that it is engaged in. They should serve not only to guide staff in their day-to-day conduct but also as a basis for making any organizational decisions. As a result, staff need to believe in them and, for the purposes of this chapter, staff need to know that one of those values reflects an insistence on ethical conduct and behaviour. They need not be elaborate or cumbersome but should instead be easily remembered and referred to regularly.

Take, for example, Walmart's number one value: "We put the customer ahead of everything else ..." This is simple and memorable for all staff. Other organizations may use a value such as, "We support life-long learning for our staff and a commitment to innovation, research, and knowledge exchange." It is simple and everyone understands what is valued and that the value won't change due to circumstances in the external environment. However, we must walk the talk.

Determining an acceptable set of values is not as easy as it appears. Clashes between what a company says and what it does are common. We so often hear about companies who proclaim the importance and value of their staff but they don't hesitate to lay off staff, freeze salaries, or expect huge amounts of unpaid overtime to be worked if it contributes more to the bottom line.

What about those who want to be seen as pillars of the community but who will close up operations if they can find better alternatives or cheaper labour in foreign countries? Consider the number of companies in recent years who have demanded government bailouts, laid off staff, rolled back wages, closed operations, or even perched on the brink of financial disaster but ultimately rewarded the CEO with huge bonuses. Doesn't that appear to be a little inconsistent?

What is important and considered a key value to some may not be the same for all. This is becoming more challenging as we face an increasingly diverse population and workforce. Ed Sullivan's values were in clear conflict with the youth of my day, and we now know whose values prevailed. The values demonstrated by some of the CEOs in the above examples were likely at odds with what they promoted to their staff, their communities, or their governments. This doesn't make one right and the other wrong, but rather the challenge becomes to satisfy all stakeholders and to have all members of the organization consistently demonstrate, by their actions and behaviours, the values so prominently posted on the organization walls and in the company's annual report.

Codes of Conduct

Codes of conduct can help promote an ethical culture as well as establish something of a moral compass for all staff. Most progressive organizations have codes of conduct in place that are intended to guide staff to ensure there is no confusion about what behaviors are acceptable. In some cases these codes are extensive, while in others they are much more concise. Regardless, one example of a code of conduct is the one found at General Electric. It reads as follows:

- Obey the applicable laws and regulations governing our business conduct worldwide.
- Be honest, fair, and trustworthy in all your GE activities and relationships.
- Avoid all conflicts of interest between work and personal affairs.
- Foster an atmosphere in which fair employment practices extend to every member of the diverse GE community.
- Strive to create a safe workplace and to protect the environment.
- Through leadership at all levels, sustain a culture where ethical conduct is recognized, valued, and exemplified by all employees.

It is simple but understandable. Please note the importance placed on trustworthiness as well as crafting an ethical culture. GE's code is part of a larger package of information that speaks to a number of ethical concerns and challenges and addresses issues such as personal commitment, compliance, improper payments, privacy, fair employment practices, insider trading, raising an integrity concern and, dealing with violations.

Other organizations take similar approaches, but almost all cover minimum standards of conduct, financial integrity and accountability, compliance with anti-bribery laws, anti-trust and competition, the importance of not defaming the employer, protection of intellectual property rights, and use of social media.

As Managers and Leaders, What Can We Do Better?

In the "Report of the Ethics Education Task Force to AACSB International's Board of Directors" in 2004, the authors noted on page 11,

> Most students will not be executives early in their careers; but they need to understand that, even as supervisors, they will play a key ethical role in the organization by influencing the daily conduct of their direct reports. Supervisors demonstrate ethical leadership through being open, fair, trustworthy, and caring with employees; by communicating about ethics and values; by role modeling ethical conduct; by focusing on means as well as ends in reward systems; and by disciplining unethical conduct when it occurs.

So, to answer the question "what can we do better?" we can simply follow the advice of this task force, intended for students in business schools but certainly applicable to all supervisors, managers, and leaders of our organizations.

I have stated many times, in writing as well as in my presentations, that each and every one of us can only be held accountable for our own behaviour. As a result, that becomes a good place to start. Therefore, one thing that all managers and leaders can do to start is to consistently make decisions that are ethically correct and, to every extent possible, that do the right thing at the right time for the right reason. But there is more.

I have made it clear that I believe every organization should have a comprehensive ethics policy/program. If your organization has one, you should become familiar with it and remind yourself, your staff, and everyone else who you have contact with that your employer has this program and that you support it wholeheartedly and expect nothing less from your staff. Notwithstanding your support in principle, there remain many shades of grey in determining ethical conduct and the rightness or wrongness of any particular action. If in doubt, it is always wise to get a second opinion from someone else, preferably somebody who you and the balance of the organization trusts completely.

If your workplace does not have an established program, there is nothing that stops you from creating your own personal or departmental code to ensure that you and your staff are adequately protected against claims of unethical behaviour. With information as readily available as it is today, primarily the result of the internet and social media, you need to be squeaky clean. Establish a code of conduct, create policies and practices regarding confidentiality and conflict of interest, and protect against workplace intimidation, harassment, and discrimination. It may help to bring the rest of the organization up to your level, and frankly your staff may just appreciate the effort and dedication to a higher ethical standard. If any staff can find fault with or fail to conduct themselves at that higher standard, it may indicate that they do not belong on your team.

As leaders and managers we must be concerned about personal characteristics such as respect, trustworthiness, and sincerity. It is important that these characteristics are exhibited by all members of the organization. Outstanding leaders reflect them in everything they do, and their staff come to expect nothing less of them. But there is more. Staff also look to see some of the following demonstrated by their managers:

- Walk the talk (already discussed at some length).
- Encourage nothing but best practices from yourself, your area of responsibility and your staff.
- Be consistent.
- Be fair.
- Be compassionate.

- Be reliable.
- Exercise self-control and always remain calm.
- Don't assign blame—the dog didn't eat your homework.

Decision-Making Tests

I believe that most people would agree with most of what I have written about ethics. The challenge comes when a person is faced with a decision that should be made in accordance with an ethical policy, and the person may not clearly see which choice is the ethical one. A. B. Carroll, in *Principles of Business Ethics: Their Role in Decision Making*, spoke of six principles to be applied when facing challenging ethical decisions. Remember, this is not an all-inclusive list. Following these six categories, I have added a few of my own. You may have others.

1. ***The Golden Rule***. Its importance as a guiding light for behaviour can never be understated. If somebody else were making the decision that you are now facing and that decision affected you, how would want them to make it? Could you respect it? Would it be ethical? Would it be the right thing to do at the right time and for the right reason? Make a decision, but always consider how you would want to be treated if roles were reversed.

2. ***Disclosure***. If you take an action, will you be comfortable if all your friends, associates and family are aware? Would you be proud, or would you be more inclined to hide your face if it became known?

3. ***Intuition***. This is not particularly something that one would consider very scientific, but it simply boils down to "What does your gut tell you about this decision?" Will you be able to sleep at night? You must always feel comfortable that it is the right thing to do.

4. ***The Categorical Imperative***. Can the principles that you apply to a decision or an action be adopted by everyone or may it force you to tell others to "do as I say and not as I do"? If I intentionally cheat on my taxes, is it okay to allow everyone else

to do likewise? If I take a pad of company paper for personal use, it is therefore all right for all my staff to do the same thing? Can I offer a friend a job but not support all my staff when they want to offer their friends and family members jobs as well? "What's good for the goose must be good for the gander" was a familiar refrain from my childhood.

5. **The Professional Ethic**. Could you support your decision if the issue came before a committee of your professional peers? How would they judge you? What would they say?

6. **The Utilitarian Principle**. If in doubt, your decisions should be aimed at doing the most good for the greatest number of people. Who gets their roads ploughed first during a winter storm? Those with the most money? The squeaky wheels? Councillors? The roads that get the most usage regardless of who lives there? Which would you choose?

I appreciate that these tests have a textbook flavour to them. However, let us remember that there are also some more practical, common-sense type tests to apply to feel better about the ethicality of our decisions. Some of those include the following:

- Would I feel comfortable if my action/decision were to appear on the front page of a major newspaper?
- Would I be proud of this decision because it will be part of my eventual legacy?
- Would my mother be proud of me? (This is the really big one, because if she is not proud of me then we have both failed. She would believe she hadn't raised me properly, and I would simply have failed to learn.)
- Would the decision be consistent with our organizational values or code of conduct?

Remember that all you can ever truly control is your own behaviour as well as the spirit, intent, and actual fashion in which it is carried out.

Make sure you walk the talk, promote ethical behaviour in others, and never be afraid to ask if this is the right thing to do at the right time and for the right reason. Pure ethical behaviour is an ideal to be aimed for, although sometimes it may appear a tad elusive. Keep practising and keep aspiring to be the best person you can possibly be.

Key Messages
The Importance of Ethics and Integrity

The Golden Rule should always guide our conduct as it tells us to "do unto others as we would have them do unto us." In part, that is where my sense of personal ethics evolved from. However, equally important, when a question of ethics arises and I make a tough decision, I always ask myself, "Would my mother be proud of this decision?"

- Always remember to do the right thing at the right time for the right reason.
- Part of being a member or even the leader of an ethical team is that you trust your staff to always do the right thing and they trust you to do likewise.
- The message that I hear most often from staff about their managers and leaders is they expect their managers to "walk the talk." If we are going to preach ethics, we must be prepared to act ethically.

Chapter 9:

Conflicts Can and Do Happen

In 1967, the Beatles wrote the song "Hello Goodbye". While the song contributed very little to a greater understanding of the nature of conflict, the tune and the lyrics became immortalized. Their words reflect a view of conflict that sees it as neither good nor bad but rather as a simple difference of opinion. As long as people have differing values, perceptions, interests and opinions, conflict will exist. Those conflicts can range from simple differences of opinion to marital disputes, an entire adversarial labour relations system and in the worst case scenario, world wars.

As we have discussed, many of our life lessons have shaped our views on management and leadership. The best approaches reflect not only good common sense but also learnings that we garnered from our parents as well as other meaningful role models. As a result, I submit that we learn early in our lives to approach conflict as avoiders, accommodators, competitors, compromisers, or collaborators. More on these types later.

My life circumstances growing up influenced how I handled conflict as an adult. Fights on any front were simply forbidden. Those were the rules that I lived by. There was no Erma Bombeck to say, in my defense, "It's simply wrong to order (kids) to stop that fighting. There are times when one child is simply defending his rights and damned well should be fighting." I became an avoider and an accommodator. Everyone is influenced by their own circumstances, and managers will need to face conflict regularly. It will be there regardless of the nature of our organization, number of staff, industry, degree of professionalism, existence of unions, or any other organizational factor, and to create a workplace where people enjoy coming to work, we must learn to manage conflict effectively.

When we put people together who are interdependent and who come from varying backgrounds, with differing values, interests, and opinions, the occasional conflict is inevitable. However, conflict does not necessarily need become negative or in any way disabling for your department or service. It can actually result in better relations, better services, and a stronger team. In large part, the magnitude of its impact on your department is up to you.

Before we talk about how to handle conflict, let's agree on a definition of conflict. For the purposes of this book, conflict is the situation that occurs when two or more parties have interests that are perceived to be competing. When faced with conflict situations, it is important that managers understand not only the respective positions of the parties but also their interests because, ultimately, that is where a true resolution is to be found.

Managers also need to understand that the cost of resolving conflict increases as its nature changes. A mild conflict between two employees, such as a difference of opinion about whether job A should be done before or after job B, generally incurs very little in the way of cost for the manager. Where that issue escalates to an open dispute over shift schedules or who will work which weekends may create serious implications for the workforce generally. Usually by this point too much time has been taken to address the issue. There is also a risk that operational efficiency will begin to suffer. As that happens, the cost of the conflict begins to increase.

If grievances are initiated, or human rights complaints registered, or lawsuits filed, the cost to address the conflict becomes burdensome. Keep this in mind and address any conflicts quickly and effectively. Don't let them grow to the point that they become open disputes.

Resolving conflict effectively depends on communication, relationships, and discipline, not just at the point of conflict but on an ongoing basis. Your ability to communicate with your staff, using the skills that I identified, will not stop their conflicts from happening. There are simply too many variables. What it will do is increase their comfort level in coming to you for help. They will know that you will listen effectively, that your door is open, and that you are approachable. They will be comfortable in speaking with you and will come to expect that you are always open, honest, and consistent. These communication skills will ultimately translate into relationship building and with solid relations having been developed with all staff and a host of others, getting to the root of conflicts will become much easier.

Finally, as I said earlier, effective management and leadership takes hard work. Nobody ever said (or if they did, they shouldn't have) that being a manager and a leader would be easy. You have to work at it and you have to be disciplined. At times you will feel like you're going to blow a gasket. Trust me, it won't help. Be disciplined, remain calm, approach conflict situations logically, and always act in the best interests of the department or service. I guarantee you that ignoring a conflict will do nothing to make it go away. Deal with it.

Constructive and Destructive Conflict

The traditional view of conflict was always that it was to be avoided at all costs. Conflict was not something that a good manager or leader faced in his or her department. It was an obvious sign of weakness. As mentioned above, when we put people together in an organization and when that workforce is as diverse as so many are, not everybody will agree with everything that their colleagues or the manager or the organization are engaged in.

A number of years ago I worked as the VP of Human Resources for a mid-size health-care facility, and the entire non-union compensation plan needed to be updated. After spending a significant amount of time, energy, and resources to develop what I felt was a great plan, I received compliments about the plan and its impact from a grand total of two of the 800 or so who were affected. Every member was positively affected by the new plan. Nobody lost any pay or benefits, but many of them felt that they deserved even more.

It led me to proclaim that I could have given everybody $10,000 more on their salary, and I guaranteed that somebody would have felt that they deserved $10,100 for some reason. We will never make everybody happy.

Conflict may be as simple as somebody complaining about their pay relative to somebody else. It could start as a complaint that Mabel didn't smile at me this morning or that Wally has bad breath or that somebody feels Lyle is drinking to excess again. I've dealt with them all and a thousand others. But these are the negative types of conflict and they need to be addressed. I have had to deal with employees with alcohol problems many times over the years. It is not easy, and on occasion the final result was somebody losing his or her job. However, before seeing that happen, I always attempt to address the matter by facing the problem head on, offering support, working with their union as necessary, looking at alternative plans, and following through. Sometimes it works and the employee regains control of their life. I have seen them become a productive member of their department once again. They have also returned to being better for their family and their community. The point is that the problem, whatever it may be, is a form of conflict or potential conflict, but that conflict can become something more positive.

Conflict is constructive when

- Everyone becomes involved in the search for a positive solution. The team grows as a result.
- Clarification and discussion of issues is encouraged. An atmosphere of openness and transparency is promoted.
- Alternative solutions are generated and explored, and a reasonable one is found.
- Emotions, anxiety levels, and stress are recognized, respected, and released in a positive fashion.
- Groups become more cohesive.
- Individual or group growth takes place.

Conflict is destructive when

- Nothing new happens and the problem remains. In other words, we fail to deal with it.
- Energy is diverted from more important tasks and obligations. We're spending so much time fighting that we're not accomplishing much else.
- Morale (individual or group) is adversely affected. Everyone is growing weary of the conflict.
- Poor self-concept is reinforced for one or more of the players involved in the conflict.
- People are divided and groups become polarized.
- It produces irresponsible behaviour as each of the participants tries to win a game of one-upmanship.

Sources of Conflict

For all the managers or those who aspire to management or leadership roles, consider the following list of conflicts and think about whether you have faced them in your area of work:

- Disagreements over resources, either lack of or how they are distributed or utilized.
- Personality clashes.
- Disputes with supervisors for a variety of reasons.
- Differences of personal standards—what can be considered to be offensive, immoral, or unacceptable behaviour.
- Questions of beliefs, including religion.
- Political conflicts—who has or is in power, what is fair, and what you may have to do to get power.
- Role clashes—who does what, is accountable to whom, and responsible for what.
- Resistance to change.
- Disputes about allocation and performance of various tasks.
- Allegations of discrimination or harassment in the workplace.
- Cross-cultural confusions—differences over attitudes, beliefs, norms, and behaviours that have cultural associations.
- Disagreements about methods of work.
- Complaints that ultimately lead to disciplinary proceedings at the workplace, at professional colleges, or other.
- Disputes over pay and working conditions.
- Meetings or groups where people cannot agree or one person wants something different than the others.
- Membership complaints.

This list has been adapted from an internal training session delivered in 2006 by representatives of the Canadian Union of Public Employees. So, for those of you out there who feel that the number-one role of some union members is to make life difficult for you, you need to be aware that their leadership face the same types of issues as what you face.

Bit of a newsflash, eh? I think this list can be condensed to a handful of key causes or drivers of conflict and Gary Furlong, writing in *The Conflict Resolution Toolbox*, refers to a model originally developed by Christopher Moore at CDR Associates of Boulder, Colorado. That model is called the Circle of Conflict. This model categorizes all conflicts into five key drivers, as follows:

1. *Relationships.* These may include past relationships with individuals ("Bob has always been out to get me") or with organizations ("the union is just out to make life difficult for me"). It may come from our own ignorance of the other party or our preconceived notions about the party based on stereotypes or something else equally misleading, such as my apple fights with the Catholic kids when we were growing up—who knows where it started? It just did, in much the same way as the dispute between the Hatfields and the McCoys.

2. *Values.* Possibly more than anything else, values are at the root of some many conflicts. Our values reflect our belief systems, what is inherently right or wrong, the differences between good and evil. Religion is one of the key areas in the values driver. Others include ethics, morality, abortion, and gay marriage.

3. *Externals/moods.* It is critical to understand, as I have said in many of my presentations, "Always be kinder than necessary to others because everybody you meet is facing some kind of a battle." Some conflicts start or are exacerbated because of unrelated issues, such as health challenges, problems at home, or financial difficulties. None of these factors may have anything to do with what is happening at work, but they may certainly affect an employee's performance, mood, or relationships with others.

4. *Data.* It has been said that we are now in the age of the knowledge worker, and because he who has the knowledge theoretically has the power, an imbalance in available information or data may lead to conflict or may hinder our

ability to resolve conflicts at work. Often, conflicts may arise as the result of invalid assumptions that are made by one or both parties about information or data.

5. *Structure.* This driver of conflict includes such challenges as a lack of resources or equipment to do a good job, the lack of authority to resolve conflicts/problems, and the conflicts that come from the organizational structure—"The Finance Department is driving us nuts," or "It's another one of those HR things," or "Why can't purchasing just get us the supplies we need? It's always such a hassle."(27)

This model of conflict seeks to understand first what the source of the conflict is. Once that is determined, we need to establish what the interests of each party are. For instance, in a dispute I was recently asked to help mediate, A felt he could not trust B and as a result believed he needed to check and double-check everything that B did. For his part, B felt that he was being micromanaged, and like most of us did not appreciate it. The problems between the two centred on their relationship and the information available or unavailable to each. There were preconceived notions about why each was behaving as they were and the lack of information that was readily available. It may have even included an element of differing values with differing perceptions about the best means of managing. However, after a couple of meetings, we determined that A was simply interested (because he was ultimately responsible) in knowing what was going on and B agreed to communicate more regularly and effectively. B only wanted to look forward to coming in to work, have fun, and be productive. He had no interest whatsoever in being difficult to work with. In fact, he wanted to be known as an outstanding employee, not a problem person. Once we were able to determine the interests of both parties, solving the conflict was easy.

Conflict Strategies

With the many sources of conflict, it is easy to see why we will face it daily. The majority of issues are quite resolvable, some more so than others. Either way, the assumption made at this juncture is that everybody involved is reasonable and interested in addressing the conflict and in making things better. The issue of toxic workplaces or difficult people or "the assholes" that Robert Sutton refers to will be dealt with later. For now, there are five strategies that managers and leaders can employ when trying to deal with conflict.

1. *Avoidance*. Like the turtle, you can declare that this is neither the time nor the place to address an issue and so, you withdraw into your shell. Other approaches for avoidance include sidestepping issues or postponing them indefinitely, believing that, in the fullness of time, they will resolve themselves. As I said earlier, on occasion, ignoring a problem may see it go away, but the more likely reality is that it will fester and worsen. Most of the time, it is best to address the issue as quickly and effectively as possible.

2. *Competing*. This is more of an issue when you are personally involved in a dispute, as opposed to having two or more of your staff involved. In this instance, the conflict becomes something of a game, where you are prepared to do anything to "win." While this may help you achieve your goals, it may also be at the expense of other parts of the organization or even at the expense of someone else's goals or feelings. Be very careful that you aren't winning the battles only to discover you will lose the war.

3. *Accommodating*. Ah, you're such a teddy bear. You are so interested in appeasing others, and to a certain extent avoiding conflict, that you are prepared to protect relationships at all costs. Confronting differences is difficult and may damage fragile feelings. I have spoken about the importance of building

and maintaining relationships, but there are ways to do that but address conflict at the same time.

4. **Compromising.** Although some see this as a good approach, it may not always be the best solution. The philosophy is that both ends are placed against the middle in the expectation that both parties give up something in order to get something. However, the best resolution may not necessarily be in the middle.

5. **Collaboration.** The central premise to this approach is that teamwork and cooperation will help everyone achieve their goals or interests while maintaining the integrity of the relationship. The process of working through differences will lead to creative solutions that will satisfy both parties' concerns.

The best resolution method is collaboration. Therefore, the essence of this section is to encourage you to build your department or service so that any disputes can be addressed via collaboration. You will increase the likelihood of engaging in collaborative actions when you

- Communicate your goals and objectives clearly and effectively. To every extent possible, involve staff in the development of those goals in order to promote further understanding.
- Encourage your staff members to engage in healthy discussion or debate that focuses on issues and interests related to their workplace rather than personalities, values, or other immaterial matters. In other words, it is okay for staff to have differing opinions. Managers and leaders need to promote the sharing of those differing opinions, the result of which is increased understanding and knowledge of one another and each particular situation.
- Promote mutual trust, respect, and support of one another.
- Provide avenues for personal/organizational growth and development. Sadly, during difficult financial times, the first

thing to fall under the axe is education and development. Try not to let that happen to your department.

- Hire for fit and for attitude. While technical skills are important, I would always prefer to have a solid team player with a good attitude than a technically superior candidate who may pull the team apart.
- Look for common solutions.
- Focus on the problem or the issues.
- Take a non-adversarial approach.
- Engage in helpful dialogue.
- Focus on everyone's interests.
- Believe that everyone can "win."
- Focus on positive change.

Don't:
- Look for someone to blame.
- Focus on personalities.
- Take an adversarial approach.
- Engage in meaningless or "ad nauseam" debate.
- Approach conflicts with a predetermined outcome in mind.
- Think somebody has to "win" and somebody has to "lose."
- Focus on control.

Dealing with Difficult People

Regardless of the source of conflict and the potential solution, people are at the heart of it. How many of us feel that there are people out there who get up in the morning intending to make our lives difficult? We all know people like that. They are toxic to the rest of us and they represent a huge burden on your department, your organization, and society as a whole. They are the staff who upset their colleagues, adversely affect productivity, and do immense harm to team unity and spirit. They cause others grief at work, and sometimes that grief spills over to the personal lives of others.

There is a cost to their bad behaviour and Christine Pearson and Christine Porath explore that cost in their book, *The Cost of Bad Behavior*. As opposed to referring to bad behaviour as "toxic," they simply look at the nature of incivility in the workplace, which they describe as "the exchange of seemingly inconsequential inconsiderate words and deeds that violate conventional norms of workplace conduct." As I noted earlier, they report that this incivility has a huge negative impact on performance of both individuals and teams and is a drain on a manager's time. It creates gross inefficiency for all of us. In fact, they have noted that job stress costs the US economy approximately $300 billion a year, much of which has been shown to be related to workplace incivility.

We have all seen the toxic personalities and those who engage in bad behaviour. We see them at work and we see them in the community. They are pushy and disrespectful. They were the school yard bullies as kids and remain abusive as adults. Temper tantrums may be regular approaches for them. Perhaps they are gossipy. We see the know-it-alls, those who are generally negative or simply whine about everything in life. There are so many other descriptors.

Have you seen these people before? Perhaps more important is, do any of these describe your own behaviour? It's difficult to see this in yourself, but you have a good, long look in the mirror, or you may be able to find out by simply asking your manager to arrange for a 360-degree evaluation, getting feedback from the manager, colleagues, and any staff who report to you, plus other stakeholders as necessary. Ask the evaluators to be absolutely honest. If you engage in bad behaviour, it will be a bitter pill to swallow, but asking for the input is a great first step.

If bad behaviour is identified as part of your makeup or if you are aware of staff in your organization who fit this description, what can you do about it?

1. Every organization should have what Sutton calls the "No Asshole Rule." You need to serve notice to every member of your organization that you will not tolerate bad behaviour and general incivility. There should be a code of conduct and a clear expression of what will and will not be tolerated.

2. All managers and leaders need to walk the talk. Create a positive climate for your service and good team spirit. You must always treat everyone with courtesy, respect, and absolute attention to an atmosphere of fairness and collaboration. You cannot be perceived to say one thing while acting in another fashion.

3. Every organization should teach courses or promote lessons in proper behaviour. Teach civility and how to recognize signs and symptoms of incivility. These lessons need not always be taught in classrooms. They can easily be conveyed in company newsletters and regular reminders found in vehicles such as company memos or paystubs. Discussing this topic during the annual performance review for all staff would be of value. Listen for evidence of incivility or bad behaviour and specifically address this as an issue in exit interviews.

4. Make sure hiring practices filter out those with patterns or a history of incivility or bad behaviour. I don't care how technically sound they are. Don't let them into your department in the first place, and if they do find a way in, get them out as soon as possible.

5. When you see evidence of incivility or bad behaviour, deal with it immediately and effectively. Make sure that the perpetrator understands what was unacceptable and what the ramifications of further incidents will be. There can be no room for that sort of conduct, or it will simply grow like a weed.

Labour Relations

The topic of labour relations deserves special attention, because for many managers, the union at the workplace is forever cast in a bad light and unfortunately it is seen as evidence of destructive conflict.

Knowing something about labour relations may help dispel some myths and encourage some better relations and reduce conflict at the same time. It should be obvious to the reader that my treatment of this part of the topic will merely scratch the surface as entire university master's programs are dedicated to labour relations. However, even a cursory review is important.

There are three aspects of labour relations about which I wish to enlighten managers and leaders: the legislative perspective, collective bargaining, and grievance handling.

The Legislative Perspective

Now, before I get started, I don't want the labour lawyers out there to come looking for my head because I'm trying to practise law. I am not. However, I have learned a few things after many years as a labour relations practitioner and consultant. I have taught labour relations courses, negotiated hundreds of collective agreements, presented at both rights and interest arbitrations, served on many boards as nominee, and appeared before numerous related tribunals. Therefore, my first disclaimer is that none of this makes me a lawyer, but it has served to educate me about what managers need to be aware of for the purposes of day-to-day labour relations. My second disclaimer is that my only knowledge is of the labour relations world in Ontario, Canada. The specific legislation varies from one province to another in Canada, and I suspect there are dramatic differences in the United States and other countries. The important thing is that you understand a little about how the laws affect your organization and its labour relations environment.

For those in Ontario, the Ontario Labour Relations Act is the guiding piece of legislation with the following purpose:

1. to establish and maintain orderly processes for collective bargaining between employers and their unions;

2. to encourage communication between employers and employees in the workplace;
3. to encourage cooperative participation of employers and unions in resolving workplace disputes; and
4. to promote the expeditious resolution of workplace disputes.

The Ontario Labour Relations Board is the administrative body that applies the rules set out in the act, and it deals with issues such as the certification process, unfair labour practices, the union's duty of fair representation, successor rights, strikes and lockouts, plus a multitude of jurisdictional disputes. As long as there are at least two employees in the workplace, they have the legal right to join a union. Once the employees have decided to join a union (there are a number of procedural rules and practices that dictate how cards can be signed, gathered, evidence of interest in membership, employer practices during campaigns, etc., but that is not the subject of this discussion) and they have been certified by the Ontario Labour Relations Board, it is time to enter into discussions for a first collective agreement.

Collective Bargaining

The collective agreement is the written contract between the union and the employer that sets out the terms and conditions of employment for the employees covered by said agreement. It also contains the rights, privileges, and duties of the employer as well as members of the bargaining unit. In Ontario, if the parties are unable to agree upon the terms for either a first collective agreement or a renewal agreement, they must follow a mandatory conciliation process. If that process is unsuccessful, a "No Board" report is generally suggested by the conciliation officer and issued by the board. Once that step has occurred and certain timelines have been met, the parties are in a legal strike or lockout position.

How does this all relate to conflict? Well, all you need to experience is one strike or lockout and you will appreciate where the conflict starts.

Bargaining can be a very civilized process where, if good relationships have been forged between the parties, discussions about new terms and conditions take place, some give and take occurs, and a new agreement results. In all my bargaining, this has not happened too often (but it has happened) because the issues are very personal to both parties. The employees are bargaining for things such as wages, benefits, shift schedules, opportunities at vacancies, leave of absence provisions, and so forth. The process will have a deeply profound effect on the economic lives and the work lives of all staff.

For the employer, for every improvement in wages and benefits, there is a cost factor and an impact on taxpayers for broader public sector employers or on the bottom line in the private sector. Emotions can run high, and a strike is never a pretty sight; things are said and feelings are hurt and relationships damaged to the point that it may take years to repair. It is a serious conflict that I am yet to be convinced anybody wins.

However, principles being what they are and people being who they are, bargaining is often a very high-stress, conflict-ridden process. Relationship building and effective communication remain the keys to successful bargaining, hopefully achieved without a strike or lockout. In the event of successful bargaining, a new collective agreement is reached with new terms and conditions of work. But remember, this is a legally binding contract and therefore, it is subject to errors, omissions, and violations, intentional or unintentional. What happens when a violation occurs?

Grievance Handling

A grievance is simply a written complaint alleging a violation/ contravention of the collective agreement. The process for filing of grievances will be found in the collective agreement and usually covers three or four or more steps, with the final step being to refer the grievance to arbitration. This final stage is a requirement imposed by law and ultimately signals that the union cannot strike because of a grievance or, in fact, any time during the term of the collective agreement. They can only process a grievance to arbitration where the decision of the arbitrator or Board of Arbitration, as the case may be, will be final and binding (unless challenged by one party or the other before the Supreme Court, which is not routine by any stretch of the imagination). At each step, it is generally required that management and union representatives meet to discuss and review the case. While there are mandatory time limits to process the grievance or to respond to it, in Ontario, arbitrators have the power to waive those time limits if deemed appropriate.

Managers may receive any one of three types of grievance—individual, group, or policy. An individual grievance is a matter that is peculiar to one person only, for example, a single employee was not paid overtime for one extra shift that he or she worked. A group grievance may occur if all employees who, for example, worked a weekend shift were allegedly not paid for it. A policy grievance deals with an issue of consequence to the entire bargaining unit. For example, if the employer decided to implement paid parking, the union could file a policy grievance.

Again, this is another type of conflict situation, and the extent of the conflict might well depend upon the nature of the grievance. Two hours of missed overtime is not likely to be too contentious, but the termination of one's employment is bound to make the situation a tad more heated.

There is need to point out to managers and leaders something that I have seen many times in my career, and that is the conflict that we face between a principle about being "right" on an issue versus being more pragmatic about the realities of taking an issue to arbitration. The first time I ever experienced this was when I was representing a hospital in Northern Ontario as they were dealing with a grievance alleging a missed shift premium.

As is often the case in these types of matters, the employee was determined to prove that the hospital should have paid him what amounted to approximately $20 in lost premium. The hospital insisted that they did nothing wrong and refused to pay the premium, stating unequivocally that, at arbitration, they would be vindicated.

I tried diligently to convince them that going to arbitration would cost them in the neighbourhood of $10,000–$15,000 in order to prove that they didn't owe $20. They were being penny wise and pound foolish. The union had the same challenge with the employee because it would cost them a similar sum of money, win or lose. I eventually reached into my pocket and offered to pay the employee his $20 if he would just drop the grievance. He agreed.

There will be times when you will face situations where your counsel may be strongly suggesting that you settle a case, even though you know in your heart that you are "right." Listen to their advice, because pursuing matters to arbitration is a long, slow, tedious, and expensive process. Individual feelings are sometimes hurt through the evidence-gathering process. Make sure you are going for the right reason. Be pragmatic about it.

Finally, with regard to labour relations, I know it may appear at times as though the local union rep is out to get you or his sole purpose in life is to make things difficult for the employer. While there are certainly reps who are jackasses, they have to also deal with managers who are jackasses too.

Remember the importance of building good relationships and fostering outstanding communications. It will help resolve a lot of disputes. In fact, it has helped me build some solid friendships over the years. The union rep has a job to do, assisting employees with their workplace challenges. You have a job to do in making your department or service function efficiently. The creation of an atmosphere of mutual respect and courtesy will make life so much easier for everyone involved. Having a union may create some unique challenges for you, but as you become more skilled in conflict resolution, you will discover that it isn't impossible, just challenging.

Key Messages
Conflicts Can and Do Happen

Like it or don't, sports are a form of conflict. Obviously, that very conflict can be positive in that very good qualities such as sportsmanship and teamwork are promoted. However, if sports get to a point where one team or any one individual is trying to hurt another, the conflict is not healthy. Keep things in perspective and understand that conflict can be productive.

1. Communication, like so many other aspects of leadership, is critical. Good communication skills can help both prevent and resolve conflict.
2. Collaboration is the best way to address conflict, as it involves elements of both teamwork and cooperation. At the same time, it aims to maintain the integrity of the relationship.
3. Remember that dealing with unions is not necessarily a bad thing and that relationships can be built. Remember also that in many grievance situations, there are principles as well as pragmatism at stake. Make sure you understand the essence of both in each individual case.

Chapter 10:

Change in the New World of Work

Flowers are red; green leaves are green,
There's no need to see flowers any other way,
Then the way they always have been seen.
—Harry Chapin, "Flowers Are Red"

As I wrote in *Common Sense Leadership*, I'm not sure if Mr. Chapin was questioning the educational system of the time or simply imploring us to open our minds to new ways of seeing things and really start colouring outside the lines. For those who don't know the song, he goes on to speak of a little boy who attends school for the first time, and part of his new experience includes a teacher who refuses to acknowledge that there is any other way than to paint flowers red and leaves green. However, he insists by saying,

> There are so many colours in the rainbow,
> So many colours in the morning sun,
> So many colours in the flowers and
> I see every one.

The teacher eventually breaks his spirit, and when he attends a new school where the new teacher is smiling and says, "Painting should be fun," his response has become, "Flowers are red and green leaves are green."

The world we live and work in is a wondrous place of infinite possibilities and opportunities. The more we are able to adapt to change, the more likely it is that we will enjoy our work. Our world has always been changing, and we have always been a part of those changes. It's just that we have forgotten how to bring about change or how to adapt to it, or even enjoy it.

Think back to your childhood. Change happened every day in every way. We were perpetually growing, physically, mentally, spiritually, and emotionally. The world changed around us as new technology generated excitement never before experienced. For me, it happened to be a colour TV instead of the old black and white model or perhaps more than just two or three channels to watch. Our parents got new jobs or we moved to new neighbourhoods or found new friends or played new sports. Then we got married or left home for new adventures. We perhaps got our own apartment or our own house, had babies, and tried new jobs ourselves. We had dreams about how great life was going to be. Things never stay the same, and yet, somewhere along the line, we sometimes tended to forget about the wondrous nature of change, choosing instead to fall into patterns and behaviours that attempt to support the status quo as that becomes the place where we are most comfortable. But we know that can never be.

What about others who have had dreams that we have seen come to pass? Martin Luther King had a dream that included whites and blacks living in a fair and just world as equals. John F. Kennedy had a dream of seeing a man landed on the moon. Bill Gates wanted a computer in every home. Speaking of computers in every home, I remember well a time when I was a vice president of a mid-sized hospital in Ontario, and one day the IT director delightedly let me know that he was having a brand-new computer placed on my desk. I told him, quite frankly, that he was wasting his time and I would refuse to even turn it on. I held good to that threat for two years. Finally, one of his staff was able to convince me that the world wouldn't stop just because I pushed the power button. It went from there.

I was terrified of something I did not know or understand. Technology is still a challenge for me. Even more frustrating, my grandchildren handle technology and its accompanying changes with absolute comfort (my two-and-a-half-year-old granddaughter knows how to work the iPad better than I do). That is what change does for many of us. For me, it's technology. For others, change in jobs or functions or marital status may be equally terrifying.

There are two overall themes I want to consider in this chapter. The first is our personal response to change; the second is the nature of organizational change and how we as managers and leaders can best bring about necessary changes in our workplace so that our staff are not as terrified as I was with that first computer.

Personal Response to Change

One of the most delightful yet helpful books I have read in recent years was *Who Moved My Cheese*, by Spencer Johnson. The book jacket describes the story best:

> Who Moved My Cheese? is a simple parable that reveals profound truths about change. It is an amusing and enlightening story of four characters who live in a "Maze" and look for "Cheese" to nourish them and make them happy.
>
> Two are mice named Sniff and Scurry. And two are "little people"—beings the size of mice who look and act a lot like people. Their names are Hem and Haw.

"Cheese" is a metaphor for what you want to have in life—whether it is a good job, a loving relationship, money, a possession, health, or spiritual peace of mind.

And "The Maze" is where you look for what you want—the organization you work in, or the family or community you live in.

In the story, the characters are faced with unexpected change. Eventually, one of them deals with it successfully, and writes what he has learned from his experience on the maze walls.(28)

There are a number of key lessons to be learned from the story and how we, as individuals, can respond to change. Those lessons include seven items.

1. Change happens

Change happens, and collectively we have to get on with it. For so many of us, when change happens, it threatens that which with we are comfortable. A new computer, a new boss, a new job routine, new demands and expectations, new legislation or policies or procedures, etc. Stop thinking of these things as problems, but rather accept that we each have the power to turn adversity into opportunity.

In Ontario, recent legislative changes have created the opportunity for full-day kindergarten in public schools. For parents, this is a godsend. However, the implications for taxpayers in general are huge. Also, by so doing, the government cut into the entire children's services industry. Private operators will lose revenue and clients. Early childhood education professionals' jobs will be threatened, or at the very least changed dramatically. Their options, at this juncture, are to stamp their feet and pout or, like Hem in *Who Moved My Cheese*, do nothing. Either course of action will not be satisfactory.

The affected professionals need to accept that change happens and now, an opportunity has been presented to create something new and wonderful. They need to turn the adversity into opportunity. I'm not sure what that will look like, but I'm not a Early Childhood Education professional. This is their chance.

2. Anticipate change

We can't become complacent. I have worked a great deal in the municipal sector. At times, municipal organizations achieve great things. However, we can expect that, every four years, with a new council in place, they will want to place their own stamp on operations and leave their own legacy. In other words, it really doesn't matter how well things are working—a new council will want to change something.

Similarly, over the years, we have heard the expression "The more things change, the more they stay the same." The provincial government in Ontario has gone, over the years that I have been exposed to them, from centralized approaches to programs and policies to a decentralized approach and back to centralized again.

With each new government, we can anticipate that there will be change coming. Things are no different in the private sector. In order to get a leg up on the competition or to develop the next great technological advancement, innovation comes front and centre, risks are taken, and change happens. It is the one great constant in both our professional and personal lives. Know your job, your profession, and your business, whatever it may be, and always anticipate change. Be ready. It will happen.

3. Monitor change

In *Common Sense Leadership*, I spoke of the importance of scanning the horizon. Leaders need to see a world that is different from the world we are in today. That doesn't make our world bad or wrong but, as noted, change is constant. As a result, we need to get past the status quo, see the big picture, and inspire those around us. We need to grab the attention, excitement, and commitment of others to join us in the drive for greater achievements and to soar to greater personal heights.

As leaders, we need to be ready to stretch our boundaries and horizons, to consider possibilities beyond our current realities. In the words heard in one famous television show, "To boldly go where no one has gone before." Regardless of the field you are functioning within, you need to be aware of your current realities and future possibilities.

You need to read professional journals, hear what the experts are saying, and solicit the input of your staff and others in the organization. Keep abreast of political, environmental, economic, and social trends and what their impact may be on you and your department. Don't wait for someone to move the cheese in order to respond. Watch for the signs along the way.

4. Adapt to change quickly

If you anticipate and monitor change, you should have no problem adapting to it as well. Someone will move the cheese, and the quicker you let go of the old cheese, the sooner you can enjoy the new cheese. Ideally, we will have a part in the changes that affect us. However, on occasion, as noted, change happens. Get used to it and adapt quickly. Don't fight it, and if at all possible make sure you and your team become more proactive and get to the front line of the changes. How I wish I had taken on that first computer I had placed on my desk and looked at it and the technology it represented as a new and exciting adventure instead of a pain in the ass! I would have been far better served and would have served as a far better leader if I had adapted to that change quickly.

5. Change

Take chances. One of the most intriguing struggles that I see many leaders endure is the fear of failure in taking risks. There are those who will tell you that we have to incorporate risk management protocols within our organizations. I have no issue with that because all it tells me is that we have to assess actions we are planning to take and what the implications of taking them may be. However, what does perplex me is that so many use this to suggest that no risk should be taken unless we know every possible outcome and what those risks may mean to the organization. That, in turn, will lead to what I referred to earlier as organizational constipation or paralysis by analysis.

We will get so hung up in analyzing risk and avoiding problems that we will do nothing, or it takes us so long to do something that we will all grow old waiting for the full and complete analysis to be done. Every invention ever considered carried an element of risk with it. Somebody had an idea that somebody else agreed was worth pursuing. Some work; some don't.

The only way we can grow as individuals, as departments, and as organizations is to take chances on occasion. They should be educated risks as opposed to wild gambles, but it is ok to take a chance and to grow. As Seneca said, "It is not because things are difficult that we do not dare. It is because we do not dare that things are difficult."

6. Enjoy the change

Savour the adventure and the taste of new cheese. I have been part of several mergers over the years and, invariably, after the changes happen, there are those who will bemoan the new order of things with comments such as, "I remember the good old days," or "It was better the way things were before." Get over it. Get out of your comfort zone and experience and enjoy the new way of doing things. Granted, things may be different, and you may in fact find them painful, but so what? In almost all instances of significant change, things are not going back to the way they were, so you might as well enjoy the ride.

This goes back to my earlier comments on the importance of attitude. When change happens, look at the glass as being half full, not half empty. The caterpillar may just become a beautiful butterfly. The ugly duckling may indeed become a regal swan. The acorn becomes a mighty oak. Enjoy each and every moment of each and every day. If you as a leader enjoy the change, there is a good possibility that your staff will as well.

7. Be ready to change again

They will keep moving the cheese, so don't get the impression that once you have adapted to one change, that's all that will happen. Nosireebob. Just as you're getting used to the new way of doing things, change will happen again. Remember that it is perpetual, so always be ready for change to happen, again and again and again.

Reactions to Change

We will never all react to or even perceive change in the same way. That is the nature of people. We are unique individuals. Knowing how to categorize how people may react to change may assist us in identifying where we, as individuals, fit, or perhaps where our staff may fit. Being so aware may help us, as managers, to understand our staff and help them deal better with organizational change initiatives.

My friend Ian Hill has identified five different reactions to change in his teachings with the American Public Works Association:

1. **Early risers.** These are the people who enjoy and thrive on change, almost purely for the sake of change itself. If a new craze is evident, they are on the front lines of the craze. Any new idea or new technology serves as their latest, great adventure.
2. **Early adapters.** They follow the early risers but at a comfortable distance. They wait until we know a little bit more about the validity of a change initiative or a new technology, and once they understand the logic they will jump on the bandwagon, even if there is still a degree of risk involved.

3. **The crowd.** Most of us land here when change has been generally proven or when a technology is not that new anymore.

4. **The legitimizers.** It takes these folks a little bit longer to catch on with the new or different stuff, because they are more careful and methodical in their evaluations. However, once they do get on board, they can be incredibly influential on those who remain resistant to the changes.

5. **The resisters.** There will always be some of these evident. Their resistance may be passive, as they just refuse to support a change or they may simply grumble about all the new things going on, or they may actively try to lobby against it prevent further change. Regardless, these are the folks who become a thorn in the side of everyone else who is diligently trying to bring a new order to things. It is to these resisters and the general theme of resistance to change that we now turn our attention.

Why Do Staff Resist Change?

Our staff may not always be as excited or as enthusiastic about change as their managers and leaders are for several reasons.

1. There are many who feel that the status quo is just fine, thank you. There will be those who have a great deal invested in the way things are—in terms of their education, experience, time (or seniority), blood, sweat, and tears. As a result, in their minds, they have a great deal invested in the way things are, and, as with any other investment, they are not necessarily eager to let go. They will need to be convinced that their investments of time and energy in the new approaches will not be wasted.

2. There is always the fear of the unknown. They need to know what the change will mean to them personally and to the nature of their jobs. They will want to know if they need to develop new skills, abilities, or methods. Will they be competent? Will they be useful still? Many folks don't look at change as a new

adventure to be faced with a spirit of enthusiasm and optimism. They remain simply afraid. We can help them become more comfortable with better communications, greater involvement in the initiative, and training. Most important, as managers and leaders, we will need to be patient. It may take some time.

3. They may not have been involved enough in discussing the change initiative or in being part of the decision-making process. As a result, there may be insufficient buy-in. "I just don't know enough about it, and therefore I'm not going to accept it." Communication, and plenty of it, is the key.

4. In a similar vein to number three above, if there has been insufficient communication about the need for the change or what it is all about, staff may fail to understand what is happening and what is needed on their part. If they don't know enough about it, they may resist the idea, no matter how valuable it may be. Communication comes into play here. If you have cultivated an open-door policy, staff will feel comfortable coming to you and asking questions. When they do, you will see where communication needs to be improved.

5. They can see no clear vision for the future. Are we changing just for the sake of change? What will our world look like when all is said and done? Share with them the nature of the overall vision and how it will improve things, not only for the company but also for them as individual staff members.

6. Some people in some organizations may face a sort of "change fatigue," where they get burned out by the perpetual state of change that occurs at their workplace. They may go along to get along but often, in this sort of circumstance, they are with us in body but not in spirit. Alternatively, if changes happen that seem to go contrary to the core values of the organization, resistance may be encountered. It is important to always keep the core values at the root of any change initiative and, to every extent possible, remember this change fatigue. Don't overdo it.

7. If we try to push a change initiative too far too fast, it may face resistance as staff are often much more capable of handling a major change one step at a time. It's like asking someone to eat an elephant. It can only be done one bite at a time. To every extent possible, be sure to implement change in small, manageable increments.

Implementing Organizational Change

We have just had a look at the reasons why staff members (including you and me) resist changes. The reasons may be very personal and unique to each one of us. However, sometimes managers and leaders make some silly assumptions but major mistakes when implementing changes in the workplace. Here are some of the things I have seen and, in some cases, some of the mistakes I have made.

1. Not everyone accepts change.

If we are contemplating a change in our organization, department, service, or structure, regardless of how important it may appear to be to us, not everyone is prepared to accept changes as readily. We can take a "father knows best" attitude, and as their leaders we may believe we know it will be in their best interests, even if it's not always obvious to them. Be prepared for the resistance that will inevitably accompany significant changes at work.

As I have already noted, different people will react in different ways. But react they will, and we need to be prepared for that. A number of years ago, while working with a large municipality, we decided, after a great deal of convincing and hand wringing at council, to build a new headquarters building. One of the reasons given for the new structure is that it would allow us to bring staff together instead of having them housed in seventy different locations. It was reasoned that they would be happier together and efficiency would increase if we weren't spending so much time travelling to one another or so much money on phone calls, mileage, etc. It was, as they say, a no-brainer. Notwithstanding the obvious benefits of the new facility, I was concerned that many staff who would be relocated there would be leaving behind many years of habits, connections with daycare, local restaurants, ride-sharing arrangements, and all manner of other connections and investments with their previous locations. I suggested a budgetary allocation of $20,000 to help with the transition to the new structure. The Council, the press, and the local taxpayers crucified me. The prevailing notion was that "they should be thankful for new facilities"; "tell them just to get to work and get on board"; "stop being so sensitive"; "quit wasting taxpayers' money on staff that are already overpaid and underworked." Fortunately, I was prepared to damn the torpedoes and found the money elsewhere, and I was able, with others, to help bring about the change process in a far more sensitive fashion than my critics believed was necessary. Remember, just because we see the value of a new way of doing things, not everyone will be as sold on it.

2. Communicate! Communicate! Communicate!

Over the years, experience has taught me that many change initiatives fail due to communications problems. Communication of messages may take on virtually every form, including face-to-face meetings, focus group sessions, newsletters, intranet messages and, of late, extensive use of social media. It's especially important to recognize and utilize the unofficial organizational leaders, who may be, whether we like it or don't, centres of influence. They may be union leaders, social leaders, or just those who happen to cross paths with almost everyone in the organization and are happy to chat with everyone they meet. We all have them, so use them to their full advantage. All messages must be multidirectional and should match the perspectives of the intended audience. In other words, a message to the board of directors will, of necessity, be different than that to the general union membership. Just remember that the overall spirit and intent of the messages must be consistent. Don't send out mixed signals. Be transparent and communicate regularly. You don't want staff to make false assumptions, fuel the rumour mill, or become angry and frustrated. After all, though we may beseech them to "not take this personally," it may have a very profound effect on them personally. Be prepared and be sensitive. Talk with them, not at them.

3. Involve the people who will be most directly and dramatically affected.

Seek their input as much as possible, especially for the aspects of change that most directly affect them. Solicit their thoughts and feelings about the extent of the changes proposed and how they can be most effectively implemented. For those who are now panicking about my suggestion that we get the feedback and input of the staff, and by doing so abdicating our responsibility as managers and leaders, fear not. Remember, your role as a leader is to make those around you better and to inspire them to greater heights. By involving them in the change initiative, you are more likely to inspire their cooperation, dedication, and energy and less likely to face as much serious opposition or resistance. Besides—and this may come as a complete shock to some—they know their jobs better than you do! They know how to bring about improvements in processes and procedures. I'm betting they talk about it all the time, but all too often we aren't listening. Listen to their concerns, give them tools and any necessary education, and above all else, be patient. Give them time to help them adjust. As leaders, the ultimate goal and the determination of that goal may be ours, but how we get there can be made far easier if we just involve the people.

4. Remember that silos exist.

Where changes are extensive enough that they cross organizational boundaries and involve more than just one department, we must be cognisant of the existence of silos. Remember that silos tend to exist in all organizations, and we will need to address that challenge where changes affect everyone. We need to promote sharing of information and resources and collaborative initiatives. There will be a need to create a transition team so make sure all affected departments are included on the team, that a common and consistent message comes from that team, and that, to every extent possible, we move forward together. It will be in the long-term best interests of the organization and is more likely to lead to a successful change initiative.

5. If changes are big ones, remember that the only way to eat an elephant is one bite at a time.

Look for small wins along the way. It may be a long and difficult journey that everybody is engaged in and every time that we achieve a small measure of success, it is important that we celebrate. In the move to a new headquarters building that I referred to earlier, all affected departments did not move in at the same time. We brought one department at a time to their new home, and as each one arrived, we arranged for an introductory welcome breakfast as well as an orientation and tour of the new facilities. By the time we arrived at the last group, the breakfast, which included all those who had already arrived, was getting big, but it was worth the effort. We considered each move to be a small win, and we celebrated accordingly. It was worth it.

Making Effective Organizational Changes

This is not meant to be an all-inclusive discussion on change management. However, we need to understand some of the aspects of change that any manager or leader needs to be aware of as they tiptoe through what otherwise may be something of a quagmire, fraught with resistance, challenges, and potential failure.

For many, it is easier to be critical of others than it is to help them improve. I am not holding myself out to be some kind of change guru. You need to attend a university like Queen's and their Change Management program to listen to the gurus. However, having attended their programs (and having received their Master Practitioner in Applied Organizational Development Certificate) and having discovered via trial and error over the course my career in leadership, I can offer the following thoughts for your consideration.

There are generally three ways to bring about organizational change.

- **Top-down:** We can use a top-down sort of model, which means we simply issue an edict and decree that things will change. This approach is quick and easy. Don't involve the people, don't communicate regularly, and expect only that the staff will do their job, get on board with the changes, be thankful for our magnificence and our kindness and just, make it work. Wrong!
- **Emergent:** Alternatively, we can take an emergent approach to change management and just go with the flow, evolve as we need to, and through continuous hope and prayer, believe that everything will unfold as it is intended to. Sometimes it works and sometimes it doesn't. Wrong again! Certainly, some changes tend to be emergent in nature because situations were unexpected or changed in a fashion different than what we envisioned when we scanned the horizon. Stuff happens.
- **Planned:** However, for any significant change to truly have a chance at success, the third approach calls for change to be well thought out, and it needs to be planned. That takes a little more time and energy.

One thing we don't want to do is to change purely for the sake of change. As I have already proposed, sometimes, while we are scanning the horizon, we are able to anticipate a new order of things. However, in far too many instances, the changes that we make are more emergent than they are planned. While the results may be adequate, the road taken to get to the final destination tends to be bumpier than it might otherwise have needed to be.

An example of an emergent change can be seen in Oshawa, Ontario. When I was growing up here, General Motors was the biggest and most important employer in the city, employing at one point more than 20,000 people. Our collective mentality was that GM would always be there and would always be the centrepiece of our economic fortunes. Times have sure changed. Though GM remains an important part of the Oshawa economic landscape, employing close to 6,000 people, it is a far cry from the "good old days." Fifty years ago, most had never contemplated this new world. However, once the truth was out there and the influence of GM began to wane, the community began to change in order to keep pace with the new reality. We have become much more focused on the education sector, employing at Durham College, UOIT and Trent University 2,000 employees and serving 22,000 students annually. The local Public School Board and Catholic School Board between them employ 11,000 staff, while various levels of government employ close to 10,000 others. Pickering and Darlington Nuclear facilities engage 6,000 staff and contribute millions to the local economy.

Other sectors have begun to grow and fill in the gaps left by the auto sector. Also, and somewhat sadly, we have become something of a bedroom community, with many taxpayers commuting daily to work in Toronto. The point is that changes in the local economy forced us to change collectively in order to survive and thrive. But it was not planned. It just happened.

I have also had the pleasure of being part of top-down approaches to change. For example, I have been part of several plans to implement paid parking at hospitals in Ontario. This is not a call to support paid parking, but the trigger in each case was lack of sufficient funding by the provincial government, which forced local hospitals to take steps to generate their own revenue. Also, as many municipalities have implemented no-smoking policies in increasingly restrictive fashions, the changes have been difficult but initiated as a result of dissatisfaction with the current situation—Public Health Units have initiated changes out of concern for the health of smokers as well as those suffering secondhand smoke. What situations have caused you or your organizations to want to make changes? You need to identify clearly the logic behind proposed changes and communicate it clearly to all affected stakeholders. It is unhealthy to implement change "just because" or because the senior leadership believes they know what is in the best interests of others.

The best approach to change is always one that is well thought out and well planned. Once we have identified the problems or dissatisfaction with the current situation, then we need to have an overall sense of where we believe we need to go for the future vision. This is the very broad notion of the future that the leader must have. It doesn't necessarily mean that he or she has to have the plan fully developed or that nobody else can be involved. However, outstanding leaders are visionary. They see the big picture and they inspire others to get on board with their vision as they grab the attention and commitment of others. Stephen Covey in *The 7 Habits of Highly Effective People* speaks of the need to begin with the end in mind. We know where we are now and if the leader has the end state in mind, all that is left is to decide how we get there.

Some of the steps that you need to take in order to make any significant change initiative successful include the following:

- As noted, we need others to get on board, get committed, and get inspired. As a result, we need to make sure others are aware of the current realities and why the current situation must change. It may revolve around funding restrictions, competition, marketplace realities, or any number of other challenges. Your staff need to know and understand these realities.
- We may need to do something akin to a SWOT (strengths, weaknesses, opportunities, threats) analysis as part of the above-noted review of current realities. So, in addition to understanding the external environment with its opportunities

and threats, we also need to understand our departmental or organizational strengths and weaknesses. In order to properly consider all of this, it becomes time to involve staff, senior leadership, and other stakeholders as appropriate. This is truly a matter of two heads (or more) being better than one.

- It is often healthy to establish a transition team, which may include an executive sponsor, members of staff, stakeholders, other departmental representatives, union input, plus outside consulting support, as needed. This is where you need to involve the organizational champions and informal leaders. There is no magic as to whom or how many may serve on such a team. However, what is critical to remember is the immense value this group can bring to the success of your project. Use this committee or team to full value, listen to their advice, and encourage them to serve (in part) as the conduit between yourself and the rest of the department and, ultimately, the rest of the organization.

- Identify the series of steps that will most effectively guide the department through the change initiative. For simple changes, it may only require two or three steps. For those that may involve restructuring or may follow mergers or something more significant, there may be many steps. As noted earlier, be patient and allow staff to absorb the full import of the change and how it may affect them. Some will be easy to convince, others less so. It is best to take your time and allow people to become comfortable with each successive step in the journey.

- I know I said it already but I'll say it again: Communicate! Communicate! Communicate! There can never be too much. Use verbal messages, memos, newsletters, e-mails, social media, and presentations at meetings. Any opportunity to deliver the message consistently, thereby reducing the impact of the rumour mill, must be used. Part of the importance of the communication process is to be transparent during the change. Without that transparency, you risk staff challenging the changes, making false assumptions, fueling the rumour mill, becoming angry and frustrated with your leadership, and simply aiming to disrupt the entire initiative. Be open, be honest, be transparent.

- As you move through significant change processes, remember that one of the myths surrounding change is that "we have smart people; they can figure this out for themselves." While that may be true, the importance of additional training during these times is as important as regular communication. Training may be needed to perform new functions, to understand new partners, customers, and routines, or to adapt to change in the workplace. Don't expect everyone to understand everything related to your change plans. Be prepared to deliver training and education to help facilitate the process.
- Remember to celebrate along the way. Enjoy the reward of the quick hits and grabbing at the low-hanging fruit of the change initiative and each time you do celebrate with your entire team.

Key Messages
Change Happens—Get Over It!

Remember when we were kids and all the changes that happened to us. We took those changes for granted as simply being part of life. We changed addresses, got older, and changed physically, met new friends, and tried new experiences almost every day of our lives. It's still happening, but we just tend to resist it a bit more.

1. Each of us has our own approach to change. Accept that change happens, adapt to it, and enjoy the ride.
2. Organizationally, make sure that you involve staff in key change initiatives and be sensitive to their reluctance to change.
3. As a leader, you must constantly scan the horizon in order to anticipate and monitor change in your environment.

Chapter 11:

Being a Better Manager through Coaching and Mentoring

I hate the term *human resources*. It seems to be too easily included with terms like *capital assets* or *fiscal resources*. We are dealing with people who are our staff members and part of our team. Every team functions better with a great coach. To that end, managers, in order to be more effective, need to be good coaches in today's world of work. One of the key benefits of being a good coach is that you will take much more pleasure from your work, from the growth of your people, and most important, they too will enjoy their work far more.

Whoever thought of their mother or father as a coach (except those who actually did coach them in little league hockey, baseball, soccer or whatever)? In reality, one role of a parent is to do that very thing. Generally, career or life coaches are there to help others see opportunities, pursue options, and most importantly ensure that they follow through on decisions and plans.

We want them to get better, but isn't that what Mom and Dad really wanted for us too? However, there are some who are now saying, "Garth, I manage this department and my role is to plan, organize, implement, delegate, and control. Making any individual staff member better is up to themselves. I can't be babysitting them all. There are just too many." My response is simple. You are not just a manager, even though that may be reflective of the duties you perform. You are also a leader, and your staff should look to you as not just the manager but also as the leader of your department. In that regard, you have a role to perform to help make employees better in a host of different ways.

That is the essence of this chapter—your role as a coach for your staff. I often reflect on the wisdom of Benjamin Zander, and so once again I will share with you his perspective of leadership, when he says that "[a conductor's] true power derives from his ability to make other people powerful." And so it is that your role as leader of a department or service, like the conductor, is to make other people, your staff, more powerful. My most satisfying times during my career have been on those occasions where I have contributed meaningfully to the growth of individual employees. This was especially true where I knew that their growth resulted from good coaching, training, and facilitation of their personal growth initiatives. I have taken concrete steps to help them become better people, better employees and, in some cases, outstanding leaders in their own right. That is how, collectively, we succeed. But first, let us consider what makes people tick, how they behave at work, and how to best motivate them. This is not intended to be a course on organizational behaviour but rather to offer some basic concepts that every manager and leader should be aware of.

Theory X or Theory Y?

In 1960, Douglas McGregor shared with the world his theory of human motivation and how managers can best approach the matter of motivating their staff. He proposed that there were two approaches that we could use, and he termed those two approaches Theory X and Theory Y. Most students who have had even the most basic courses in post-secondary education are familiar with these concepts, but for those who may not be familiar and need a brief refresher, the basic tenets of each are as follows:

Theory X suggests

- Employees inherently dislike work and will do everything possible to avoid it.
- Employees must be coerced, controlled, or threatened with punishment to make them more productive.
- Employees will generally avoid responsibility and only act with formal direction to do so.
- Most workers place security above all else when it comes to knowing what they want from the workplace.
- Employees display little ambition.
- They resist change.
- Generally, people are not really that intelligent.

Theory Y suggests

- Employees often view work as being as natural as play.
- People will exercise self-direction and self-control if committed to the workplace.
- The average person can learn to accept and even seek responsibility.
- The ability to make innovative decisions or offer creative solutions can be easily dispersed throughout the entire organization.

Unfortunately, far too many managers, especially in unionized settings, still lean toward the Theory X type of attitude. This presents a problem: if we drive people like rented mules and always expect negativity from them, we will get exactly what we expect from them. However, if our management and leadership practices align with Theory Y, we will enjoy the fruits of those efforts. Theory X pushes us toward being managers only. Being only a manager isn't going to make the changes we hope for in our workplace culture or truly make a difference for us or our employees. Theory X encourages the grind of work so many of us want to avoid. On the other hand, Theory Y wants us to be leaders as well, and one of the roles of a leader is to be a coach for her people.

We Know You're a Great Manager, but Are You a Great Coach?

Your staff are your team. As a manager, it is incumbent upon you to manage (and hopefully improve) their performance. Years ago, that meant going through a process to identify their strengths and weaknesses and telling them how you expected them to improve their performance in the future. Today's manager has the same responsibility but serves more as a coach and less as the ruler of the department. So, how do we become good coaches? Will this automatically require a return to school?

While I am the first to promote continuing education, the reality is that you don't need a certificate or fancy documents to prove that you are a great coach. Good coaching involves working with your staff to not only do the job right every time but also, to develop each individual such that they are able to continuously grow and develop as professionals and as people. Remember, the role of a manager is to engage in activities such as planning, organizing, implementing, delegating, measuring, and controlling. With that in mind and knowing that, in addition to being a manager, you need to be a leader, which involves, in large part, being a coach to your staff, what are the roles that a coach plays? If you simply consider what you believe to be the role of a professional sport coach, you may gain a sense for your own role. The roles or activities that you will be engaged in include the following:

- **Trainer.** All too often, as I have already mentioned, especially when in a tight budget year, one of the first things to be sacrificed is the education budget. Training and development budget lines are reduced or eliminated altogether. It is incredibly shortsighted, but we've all been there. Notwithstanding the organizational approach to this critical activity, nothing takes away from the importance of your role as coach to deliver training to your staff. Remember that a leader is there to make those around her better. So it is with your staff. You must be constantly alert to ways that you can make your staff better. You don't always get to pass that responsibility off to outside experts, courses, or even the HR department. This is one of your roles as coach.

- **Counsellor**. It's a fine line that we sometimes walk, knowing our staff as individuals but being ever alert to not intruding in their personal lives. Nonetheless, staff will know that, if you are a good coach, they can come to you with their issues, work related or personal. It doesn't mean you need to be a professional counsellor, but be prepared to assist them in any way you can. It may only require an open door and a sympathetic ear and heart. Sometimes, something as simple as scheduling flexibility may be all they need. Do what you can to help and it will come back to reward you many times over.

- **Mentor**. Ideally, your staff should see you as a wise and trusted advisor. I'm not so naïve as to believe that everyone will always see us in that light, but indeed, we should be a mentor, especially for those members of the team who are newer or younger.

- **Tutor**. Like your role as a trainer, being a tutor simply means spending time with individuals to help with learnings that occur outside the workplace or at least outside the department.

- **Facilitator**. Occasionally, staff may come to you for help in areas that you may initially feel have nothing to do with you. Though officially, that may be true, it behoves you to at least do what you can to assist them. Over the years I have had staff come to me wanting to explore opportunities in other departments or even with other organizations. My response could have been that it had nothing to me, the department or their job, and leave it at that. However, invariably, I would do what I could to help them gather information, arrange meetings or interviews, or even act as a reference. I see it as simply facilitating their growth as individuals and as members of the organization. While it may result in their leaving me, it may serve a greater purpose if they are going to another department. If they are going to another employer, then I simply wish them well. At least they can go speaking well of me and the organization they have just left. Life's like that.

- **Advisor.** It should seem obvious by now that this role involves providing advice to your staff as requested, as needed and as appropriate. Make time for them. They deserve it.
- **Sounding board.** Over the years, many folks have spoken to me about having an open-door policy. That is a good thing. In fact, as one person told me, "Have a reason to close your door, not a reason to open it." With the open door, you invite staff in to talk to you, and in turn you can better understand them and their issues and they feel more comfortable with you. However, if you have an open door, you need make it clear by your demeanour and your own attitude that you are approachable and available. There are those who have an open door, but the growl received by staff when they enter that open door does not exactly convey warm and fuzzies.

So What Really Motivates Staff?

When I was a young lad, probably in prime years as far as hockey development goes, I believed deep down that a career in the sport might be in the cards for me. However, my decision to go to the family cottage for the Thanksgiving weekend instead of staying home to attend twice-a-day practices all weekend was perhaps limiting for my career. And yet there remained hope.

The coach sent a message to me via one of my teammates that went something like, "You tell that *^%*_#@ son of a b----- that if he isn't here on the ice on Tuesday night, he shouldn't bother coming back." Needless to say, professional hockey was suddenly not a very realistic possibility. Added to this threat was my father's sage counsel that "only one in a million will be a Bobby Hull, and you aren't it." Wasn't that encouraging? Threats weren't working on me and my own family wasn't overly positive about the prospects, nor were they overly supportive in that regard. These same lessons can be applied to work.

Threatening staff seldom works. At best, it brings about temporary action (regardless whether or not you subscribe to a Theory X style of leadership), and a well-timed ego deflating comment is also seldom helpful to the cause. What is a manager to do?

In Thomas G. Crane's *The Heart of Coaching,* Crane reflects on a study conducted by Glenn Tobe and Associates that found that managers and employees had differing perceptions of what was important in the workplace. Employees listed as their top three motivators (1) being appreciated, (2) feeling "in" on things, and (3) an understanding attitude. These three, considered so important by staff, were ranked eighth, ninth, and tenth by the managers. For their part, the study found that the managers believed the top three motivators would be good wages, job security, and promotional opportunities.(29)

In my mind, these results hit the nail right on the head. In fact, the results of exit interviews conducted over the years at one of my former employers found, almost invariably, that staff seldom leave an employer because of pay or benefits. Instead, they leave the organization when they believe that it does not reflect a positive work environment or when they feel a lack of respect and a lack of appreciation are demonstrated by the departmental leadership.

At a time when so many employers speak so much about the challenges of recruitment and retention, it's amazing how many still don't get it. They don't understand what elements of the workplace will keep employees happy, motivated, and committed to their employer. Throwing more money at them just doesn't cut it anymore.

Again, I don't want this to become a textbook analysis of motivational theories, but there are some things that managers need to know about their staff and the nature of their behaviour at work. The two key themes seemingly at odds with each other, in this entire situation, revolve around rewards and recognition. Balance becomes the key.

Reward and Recognition

Reward and recognition have two distinct meanings, but unfortunately, and far too often, they are almost always used to convey one single meaning. First, let us consider the nature of rewards. For staff, rewards come most commonly in the form of wages and benefits. They are compensated for their service.

However, once we consider the "merit," we begin to move into a new domain. In consideration of meritorious service, however that may be defined, we offer additional rewards such as bonuses or even the gold watch for 25 years of service, or perhaps a special award for particularly outstanding effort or innovation or community service. For bonuses to be effective, they need to be directly linked to the behaviour being rewarded. In addition, they must be timely and equally available for everyone, and all staff must know the exact nature of the plan. Remember that, as a manager, one of your roles is to serve as coach with the intent to improve the performance of your staff. Financial rewards, if given out properly, can serve that purpose.

As for the long service awards, there are many versions, and while the intent is always a noble one, recognizing and showing appreciation for many years of loyal and dedicated service, too often they merely reflect that the employee has managed to keep attending work for 25 years ("I have managed to survive here that long"). What we really want to achieve is to have staff fully engaged in their work every day that they come to work. For that, the day-to-day recognition is of far greater consequence for you as their manager and coach.

Curiously enough, on one hand, day-to-day recognition is easy. On the other hand, we miss the boat so many times in so many ways. The easy part must start with the premise that the majority of your staff are honest, trustworthy, hardworking, loyal people. While I grant you that there are always exceptions, you need to be able to trust most of your staff. If you can't do that, you have a serious problem that requires more than this book can deliver.

However, I don't believe that to be the case, and as a result, another lesson from our youth comes into play, a lesson that too many of us too quickly forget. When somebody does something for you, say "Thank you." That's easy. I know your staff are paid to work, but you don't want them to just work. You want and need them fully engaged in what they do. Say thank you. Encourage them to regularly thank each other. Build a culture whereby everybody is happy to recognize each other for jobs well done. Not only should we be happy to thank each other but we should feel comfortable telling one another when a job, chore or project is well done. It starts from the top, and you need to build it into your daily relations.

As managers who also coach, it's incumbent upon each of us to foster a culture of recognition. You may be unable to influence the entire organization or the whole community, but you can certainly exercise influence on your department or service in order to make a difference. What is most important is that you lead by example. Make sure your glass is always half full. View your staff as individuals, and remember to be kinder than necessary, because everyone you meet is fighting some kind of battle.

I cannot stress this enough. I can almost guarantee that we all know people that are having marital problems, financial difficulties, challenges with kids, personal health issues, and a host of other things they need to deal with every day. They may not speak about it, but we all face it at one time or another. Don't lose sight of that fact in your daily interactions with your staff. Thanks are important and recognition for outstanding work or effort is critical, but it must be sincere and appropriate. It should generate interest and enthusiasm among the staff. A good recognition program is something we can all promote. It can be easy, it can be inexpensive, it can build team spirit, and it can contribute meaningfully to everyone's job enjoyment. It's all part of good coaching.

Performance Management

A brief word needs to be said about this topic and its role in coaching. Remember, this is coming from an HR guy. In most larger organizations, the HR department will work diligently—and for very good reasons—to promote organization-wide consistency in performance management programs. They will push departments to meet regularly with staff, set goals, evaluate progress, and act to deal with individuals when performance standards are not being met. This is all well and fine. However, all too often, these programs fail to meet some reasonably basic tests, the most basic of which is, are they serving to improve overall performance?

Let me state for the record that I really don't care about the nature of performance management programs. I have seen the "cookie cutter" approaches and the most elaborate systems known to mankind, 30 or 40 pages of useless information. In most cases, managers are loath to engage in these programs mainly because they "have better things to do." Managers and staff are often opposed to the process. How do we make it easier for everyone involved?

Years ago, I came across a suggestion that the ideal annual performance evaluation was one that simply asked four key questions:

1. What have you accomplished this year?
2. What could you have done better?
3. What are your goals for next year?
4. How will you improve yourself?

There is no magic to these questions. The point is that once they have been asked and once you have agreed upon where the staff member is headed for the upcoming year, the really important part of the process is the discussion phase. Have regular chats with each staff member that reports to you to consider the good, the bad, and the ugly about their performance. Quit worrying about the forms that some schmuck in HR is demanding be filled out. If your organization is not big enough to warrant having an HR department, have these discussions on your own. Either way, the important thing is that communication happens. The staff member knows you are watching, you are caring, and you are there to help. That's all that really matters.

Coaching Models

Sometimes it is hard to know where to start when trying to implement coaching as part of your management style. I have reflected on the following two models of coaching because they are relatively simple to apply in any business, organization, or industry. There may be others, or perhaps there are elements of both that may be useful. What is particularly important is the coaching activities associated with each. Use them as you see fit.

GROW

In Sir John Whitmore's book, *Coaching for Performance,* he champions a coaching model that is simple to use and yet applicable to virtually every level of every organization. So, in addition to performing all the various coaching roles that have been identified so far, it is possible to take things one step further and apply the GROW model to individual staff members. GROW is an acronym that stands for Goals, Reality, Options, and What (will you do).

Step 1
Identifies and clarifies the type of goal being pursued following a discussion with a staff member. It considers any ultimate goals,

performance goals to be established, as well as progress checks along the way. This step outlines the employee's aims and aspirations and clarifies the desired results.

Some of the questions that may be asked in this step may include the following:

- Where do you see yourself in five years? This may be in terms of job or personal aspirations.
- Do you consider this to be a stretch goal? How challenging will it be?
- If you get there, so what? What benefits will there be for you?
- How will you measure the success or lack thereof?

Step 2

This step takes time to allow the coach and the employee to assess the realities facing the employee on the road to the achievement of their goals. It may include clarifying the results and effects of previous actions or simply providing clarity about internal or external obstacles and blocks to be faced. I may set as a goal for myself that I want to now become a neurosurgeon. However, a good coach will ensure that I am realistic in knowing what the realities possibly blocking that goal are—I'm too old to start down that road, my education background is not a fit for that goal, and it takes a huge amount of time, money, and energy that I may not have. This example is perhaps a little silly, but it may help in the understanding.

Assessment of this step will include the following considerations:

- We know where you want to be in five years. How would you describe where you are now?
- What challenges may you face if you head down this road?
- What support may you get from your friends, family, or colleagues?

- Have you considered this sort of goal previously? What happened? What went right and what went wrong?
- What other realities do we need to consider (financial, social, time pressures, etc.)?
- Do you see any other roadblocks, and if so, what will it take to remove them or get around them?

Step 3

This step encourages the employee to look at the options available to him. Remembering where he eventually wants to go, as identified in the first step, we can now help him identify different possibilities.

- What are the pros and cons of each option considered?
- Which one will you choose?
- Why did you select this option? What makes it most appealing?
- If this one doesn't work out, what else may you consider?
- Is the chosen option considered realistic or just desirable?

Step 4

This is the action step and simply asks the employee, "What will you do?" Staff are encouraged to consider what they have learned through the process to date and how they will use that information to establish an appropriate plan of action, as well as any steps along the way. This step highlights the necessary commitment, accountability for action as well as any measures that let us know how they are doing. For the coach's part, it may spell out what support or development may be needed as well as any potential actions on the part of yourself.

- What will your plan of action look like?
- Where will you start? When?
- Identify all the real and potential obstacles.

- Who else needs to be involved and why?
- What will their roles be?
- What support do you need and who will you get it from?
- How committed are you to this goal?

These are not predetermined questions but rather the type of question you may wish to consider as you assume a role of coach for your staff. There may be thousands of others. It would be inadvisable to get into a box where you take a cookie cutter approach and always ask the same questions in every situation. Ideally, if you are coaching staff, the conversations need to be comfortable and free flowing, not stilted.

Transformational Coaching

The second model that I will consider, transformational coaching, is simply another approach to coaching staff. As defined by Thomas G. Crane, it is "the art of assisting people enhance their effectiveness, in a way they feel helped." As with other models, the goal is to take a coachee from where he or she is currently to a place that is considered better in his or her mind, whether professionally or personally. Crane identifies seven key elements of a transformational coach. Do any of these sound familiar? The coach must

- Invest time to get to know people as people.
- Understand people's roles, goals, and challenges on the job to be helpful.
- Set clear context and future expectations.
- Observe people's work closely enough to have relevant and substantive feedback.
- Provide timely, candid, and specific feedback regarding what you observe and interpret as the impact on yourself, other people, and performance.
- Stimulate learning, growth, and performance improvement by asking effective learning questions—offer suggestions as necessary.

- Leave people feeling supported and empowered to contribute at increasingly higher levels.

My advice to every manager and leader out there is to not worry about following any one model of coaching to the letter. More importantly, understand that in today's world, we don't lead by simply fulfilling our roles as manager. We now need to act as coaches, cheerleaders, facilitators, sounding boards, and trainers. Ultimately, one of our key roles is to make those around us better in every way in the work they do and the lives they lead. You can create your own model.

Even though we have covered models of coaching and what motivates staff, how do you best fulfill these coaching roles?

1. **Know your people intimately.** This doesn't mean that you party with them every weekend or that you exchange gifts with them on their birthdays or that you are otherwise joined at the hip. What it means is that you know them as individuals. You understand that they have issues to deal with at home, or perhaps they are struggling with health issues, parental matters, or child care arrangements. One way you can do this is by engaging in the practice of MBWA—management by walking around. Regularly walk through the department or the plant and ask individuals how they are doing. Engage them in conversation about things other than work. Eventually, they reveal details that allow you to know them as individuals so at some point, when you walk through the plant, you are able to say, "Good morning. How are you coming along with the new cottage?" or "How is you mother feeling these days?" or perhaps "Is the new babysitter working out for you?" You don't need to intrude on their personal lives and space, and by no means do you press those who wish to remain private, but knowing them as individuals and not just human resources will allow you to become a much better coach and manager.

2. **Be an outstanding role model.** The importance of acting as a good role model can never be underestimated. You can never have as your operating mantra "do as I say, not as I do." If I want my staff to have fun at work, I had better make sure I'm having fun. If I want them to set goals for personal and professional development, I must do likewise. If I expect them to be customer focused, then I must be as well. You get the picture. However, one part of being a good role model is accepting that you don't know everything about everything and nor can you ever hope to. If you accept that you are not perfect and that you are prepared to listen to the ideas and input of your staff, you can easily become a far better and more effective manager, coach, and leader.

3. **Set high standards and high expectations.** Although we can accept that we aren't perfect, we should set high standards and high expectations for ourselves, especially if we have high expectations for our staff. This applies to every aspect of our performance and the way we present ourselves. As laid back as I have always been, in an office setting, I still have expectations that staff will dress and appear professional at all times, even on "dress down Fridays." As a result, I don't want them to show up for work with holes in old blue jeans or dirty, ratty-looking clothes. At the same time that I don't want them to appear unprofessional, I cannot allow myself any lesser standard. The same is true of my interactions and relations with colleagues, staff, and the community at large. What I expect of my staff, I must deliver myself. Be a good role model and at all times "walk the talk."

4. **Set goals for yourself, your team, and each individual on the team.** I know this goes back to the performance management discussion, but a large part of this process includes the clear communication of your goals and team goals to everyone. For years, I would share both my personal and departmental goals (developed with the input of all staff) with all staff. It usually

came in the form of a state of the nation sort of memo that I sent to my boss. It was easy after that to simply copy everybody, thereby assuring complete transparency. Whatever the goals are, make sure that they remain challenging but realistic. In other words, don't declare, "We will increase production by 20 percent at the same time we cut costs by 50 percent." That sort of thing goes well beyond challenging and is not likely very realistic. Be sensitive to what is possible and develop action plans that support those goals.

5. **Develop plans that align with your goals.** The goals and action plans that you set should be done with the input of staff and should be specific, measurable, realistic, and time oriented. Eventually, we will need (consistent with performance management principles) to measure our collective and individual accomplishments so think about that when setting the goals. Involve the staff. As coach, you need to achieve some agreement with staff on what the goals will be and how we will know if we have met them. For a professional hockey coach, the measures may include things like more wins, more goals for, and fewer against, as well as individual goals such as total points, improved goals against average, or an improved plus/minus record. Those things are all measurable. Do the same with your staff.

6. **Give feedback.** Staff need feedback on their performance, and most often it needs to come from their leader. While feedback can be given as part of the goal setting, performance management process, a good coach will also provide feedback on a more regular and consistent basis. As a result, when good things happen, make sure you tell them about it. There is nothing more powerful than immediate and positive feedback on a job well done. Similarly, when something goes wrong, make sure they understand what happened, why it happened, and how we can prevent it from happening again in the future. Be specific and be helpful. Use every opportunity to make

negative situations true learning experiences. Find the silver linings wherever possible. Be helpful and remember that one of your roles is to develop people. This is just one way of doing so.

7. **Empower your staff.** I spoke earlier about wanting to ensure that our staff are fully engaged in their jobs. One way to get to that ideal is to not micromanage staff but instead to empower them. This means only that, as Robin Sharma says, we encourage them to be the CEO of their own job. We encourage them to take ownership of those things for which they are responsible. Some of my former managers, leaders, and mentors would say things like, "Don't bring me problems; bring me solutions." This doesn't mean abandoning staff but rather letting them take charge of those things they are more than capable of taking charge for and giving them the necessary advice, counsel, guidance, and support. Trust them. Don't micromanage. Mistakes will happen, but that's all part of the learning process. Give them what they need to succeed, but that doesn't mean doing their job for them.

8. **When problems occur, deal with them.** Stuff happens. Deal with it. We don't live in a perfect world, and not everybody is golden or perhaps as loyal and dedicated as the rest of us. Recruitment mistakes are made. As a result, there are times when coaching won't help. Be prepared for that possibility. As a last resort, we may have to remove some players from the team. If that is necessary, do it.

Above all else, be a good listener and a good communicator. Remember that the good Lord gave us two ears and one mouth so we could listen twice as much as we talked. As much as possible, use face-to-face communications when coaching staff. E-mail, voice mail, Twitter, and Facebook are all well and fine and may be good tools, but they don't replace face-to-face contact. Try not to forget this in your dealings with staff.

> ### *Key Messages*
> ### *Managers and Mothers as Coaches and Mentors*
>
> As kids, our parents were filled with enthusiasm for us and for our potential to grow up to be good people, always striving to make us the best we could possibly be. No matter how good we were, they recognized that there was always potential to make us even better.
>
> 1. Remember to know your staff as individuals, not just human resources.
> 2. Always be an outstanding role model.
> 3. Set high standards for yourself and great expectations for others.
> 4. Worry less about forms and systems and worry more about having regular discussions with each staff member. Your role as a coach is to make them better as employees and as people.

Chapter 12:

Alternative Work Arrangements

I want to encourage organizational managers and leaders not only to enjoy your work (and quit your job) but also to allow your staff to enjoy their work. Over the years, as I have had the opportunity to work with managers organizing their workloads, addressing staff issues, and helping resolve scheduling problems, I have regularly faced both implicit and explicit resistance from many of those managers to the consideration of new and different approaches to work. Instead, they regularly lean on what they believe to be the "tried and true" approaches.

However, today, we face a different work world where the "tried and true" may cause us to stumble out of the blocks. The only life lesson that can possibly be applied to these situations are the ones where moms and dads have forever been encouraging their kids to "at least try it" (usually applied to something like eating liver or onions or oysters or anything else that kids may consider to be "yucky").

There are two key factors that need to be considered when contemplating the use of alternative work arrangements. First, at least try some of the new arrangements, which I will describe in more detail to follow.

Second, for many of these newer approaches, an element of trust is required. I have spoken to the importance of trust in employment relationships, and this is another example of where that trust can be used to significant advantage.

Why Change Now?

For those who steadfastly refuse to change the nature of employment for themselves or their staff, they forget that the conditions that were evident when we first created the five-day/forty-hour workweek (or some variation thereof) are not necessarily the same conditions that exist today, nor are they similar to those we appear to be headed for in the future. How are they different?

First, 30 or 40 years ago, most families had only one parent in the workforce and one parent staying at home. It was the stay-at-home parent (usually the mother) who had responsibility for any childcare, elder care, or any other "home"-related matters to be dealt with. In today's world, in the vast majority of cases, there are very few stay-at-home parents, as most are in the workforce. As a result, there is not only increasing pressure on staff to attend work regularly, but those same staff members may have to look after domestic matters. This is still particularly the case for women more than men, as they continue to shoulder the bulk of home-related duties.

Second, this is the first time in our history that we have had four generations all working side by side with one another. The veterans (born 1922–1945) have suddenly discovered that they have the ability to continue working or may need to or simply want to. This has been aided somewhat by the elimination of mandatory retirement in many jurisdictions. People can now work well past the age of 65. Meanwhile, baby boomers (1946–1964) continue to occupy the biggest chunk of the workforce. The children of baby boomers (Generation X, 1965–1980) represent what we used to call the "up and comers," while Generation Y (1981–2000) have just begun to enter the workforce.

While, in and of itself, having four generations working together would not be considered as problematic, they have huge differences when it comes to their respective views of work. I want to emphasize that these are broad generalities, and every reader will no doubt be able to find exceptions to these rules. However, I believe the generalities can be borne out in the majority of cases.

- The veterans in the workplace generally respect hard work, loyalty, and a command-and-control environment.
- Baby boomers feel that home problems belong at home, not at work. Boomers have leaned more toward being workaholics, looking at work as a huge career opportunity. They love their meetings and look to be consensual leaders. They have not been as concerned about work/life balance, because work always comes first anyway.
- Gen Xers just aren't that thrilled with work, and they demand balance in their lives. They perpetually challenge authority and really don't want structure in terms of their workplace.
- The Gen Yers want to do as much as possible electronically, which translates into instant gratification without too much consideration of manual labour. Balance again is important in their lives.

The result of these generational differences is that, as a manager and leader, you will discover that the approach taken for one age group does not automatically translate into the norm for all age groups. It becomes a case of "different strokes for different folks." Not all staff will be enamoured with the notion of working 40 hours a week for 40 years of their lives.

While some baby boomers wear the fact that they work huge amounts of overtime as some kind of badge of honour, the next generations are simply saying "no thanks" to overtime, and we are now hearing things like, "I would actually rather work fewer hours if possible, or maybe work from home occasionally." That's interesting.

Third, organizations of all types in all industries and settings like to believe that "every day, in every way, we're getting better and better." The translation of this is that we want to increase our workload and productivity at the same time that we try to downsize our workforce or streamline the means of production. The result is that stress levels for all staff are growing in leaps and bounds. In the *Voices of Canadians: Seeking Work-Life Balance*, Dr. Duxbury et al. pointed out these challenges as follows:

> What are the problems at the organizational level? High workloads due to downsizing, unrealistic expectations, a lack of planning and priorities, a lack of resources, and office technology. An organizational culture that does not support balance (e.g., focus on hours, focus on money). Organizational changes such as downsizing, restructuring, and amalgamating that increase workloads and work stress and decrease job security. Upper management who are not supportive of work-life balance and an immediate manager who is non-supportive.

> The personal and family circumstances that Canadians identified as being problematic included the death of a family member, divorce or separation, being a parent or step-parent, having responsibility for eldercare, lack of support within the community, physical or mental health problems, lack of time for personal or family roles, caring for a disabled dependant, and having both children and eldercare responsibilities. The comments suggest that many of the issues on the family side of the work-life equation are more transient in nature and depend on one's stage in life. In other words, employees need different types of support at different points in their life. This

suggestion reinforces the need for flexibility at work and within the community.(30)

The key line in this entire section is "employees need different types of support at different points in their life," and we are not all at the same point in life. Therefore, a hard and fast work schedule or a one-size-fits-all approach to work is not likely to be a satisfactory approach in this day and age. It may be time to become more flexible.

Benefits of Flexibility
Believe it or not, there are benefits to be achieved by workplaces for offering flexible work schedules to employees, and there are obvious benefits for the employees. The benefits for workplaces include improved attraction and retention capabilities as well as reduced absenteeism. For employees, flexibility allows them to better manage home responsibilities and increased job satisfaction as well as an improved ability to handle stress.

Attraction and retention
It's becoming a bit of a dog-eat-dog world out there as far as attracting and keeping good staff. As I've already noted, the younger folks don't feel the same employer loyalty that earlier generations did. They are more likely to go where they feel the work atmosphere or arrangements may be more to their liking. While that may not mean that a manager has to pander to their every need, she does have to look at the bigger picture to decide what costs come with recruitment initiatives, turnover, and general dissatisfaction. You need to remember that recruitment costs money. That may be in lost productivity with new staff, the loss of intellectual capital from departing staff, the cost of recruitment initiatives generally (estimates range from 1.5–2 times the annual salary of the position being advertised), time, and energy spent on preparing job specs, reviewing resumes, and interviewing.

In addition to these costs, for some positions, there aren't enough qualified people out there to fill every vacancy. As I noted earlier, we are entering a period in our history when we will soon have to rely on immigration to fill our recruitment needs. The last thing we want is to lose good staff or to have those people currently on staff to be disengaged because we refuse to consider new alternatives to getting the work done. If we can reduce the amount of turnover and keep good staff who are fully engaged by looking at new and different ways to get the work done, would it not seem advisable to do so?

Reduced absenteeism

I've spoken about the importance of having fun at work and its impact on reducing absenteeism. Being flexible in our work arrangements is akin to having fun. It makes the workplace more meaningful for staff, who then tend to be more loyal and concerned about things like the cost of absenteeism. If you work for an organization that has 200 staff and a budget of $10 million dollars, an even nominal absenteeism rate of 3 percent is costing the organization $300,000 a year if the absent employees receive full pay for the days missed. If they must be replaced with staff receiving overtime rates of pay, the impact is even greater. This doesn't consider things like lost productivity or the adverse impact on employees to have to cover for their colleagues.

Almost every employee is ill on occasion. Organizations accept that fact. However, it becomes more problematic when employees are not just sick but they absent themselves from work in order to deal with domestic issues. Again, if we can be flexible enough that employees are able to address these home issues without being absent from work, are we not better served because of it?

Managing home responsibilities

Most of us, at one time or another, must deal with elderly parents who need to go to the hospital or to see medical professionals, kids who are sick and can't go to school, grandchildren who need help for the day, the plumber is coming over and someone needs to be there, the car won't start, the dog has to go to the vet, the need to write papers or exams for continuing education programs, or myriad other personal challenges.

It would help dramatically if we could simply flex our time in order to both address those needs and do our job at the same time. With technology at the level it is currently at and getting better all the time, how many of us could be working from home while the plumber did his thing or while we were waiting for the doctor to see Mom?

As I write this section, I'm sitting in my office at home with sweatpants and a T-shirt on. Would I be better able to work if I attended an office out of my home instead? Of course not. The more flexibility we can build into our collective personal schedules to the extent that we benefit and the employer is not adversely affected, the better served we all are. Talk about a win-win scenario. I can think of nothing better.

Increased job satisfaction and stress management
I've already alluded to the possibility that employees who are given additional flexibility in either their schedules or work arrangements will be more satisfied, as they may be better able to handle home responsibilities. If that's true, is it not also true that they will enjoy their job more? If they enjoy their job more and can look after home responsibilities more effectively, will their stress levels not decline? If their stress levels decline, is it not true that their health will generally be better and therefore, will be less of a drain on the health-care system? The obvious answer to all these questions is a simple yes, and yet we still spend too much time and energy resisting new and different work arrangements. Let us create a workplace where we can have fun, enjoy greater job satisfaction, get the job done, and be collectively less stressed.

Alternative Work Arrangements

The following represents a sampling of approaches, but there may be others, or they just may not be labelled as anything special. Keep an open mind and remember that ultimately, I want all people to be fully engaged in and enjoy their work, but they need to be productive (measured in a variety of ways, be it the number of widgets manufactured, calls responded to, reports written, computer problems solved, etc.). Those are the only two measures that are important. Notwithstanding these simple measures, we must also remember that not every job lends itself to any of these options. For example, the role of an RN in the local hospital is to look after patients. She's not likely able to do her job by telecommuting in this instance (although organizations such as Ontario Telehealth do so quite impressively). Also, not every member of staff will be enamored with alternative work arrangements. Particularly some of your older staff members may be particularly sensitive to "this new age stuff." They don't want anything but the regular schedule and may not see the value in it for others. Regardless, my key message is to be open to options, be flexible and, to every extent possible, practise good servant leadership.

- **Flexible working hours.** This is one of the easier arrangements to implement, as it involves continuing to work, for example, an eight-hour day, five days a week, but each day may not always start or stop at a given time. In many instances, all employees are required to be at their stations for a given set of "core hours" but can vary the rest of their day according to their own needs. It could be that the employer needs all staff to be present between 9:30 and 3:30, but any one employee may start anytime between 7:30 and 9:30 and finish their day between 3:30 and 5:30. In most cases, the start time and the finish time is known and agreed to in advance, but that doesn't mean absolute flexibility is not allowed. A staff member may need to juggle his or her schedule to coordinate with a spouse and children to respond to daycare needs or even to coordinate with another member of staff. As a result, he or she may start at 7:30 on Monday and Tuesday, finishing at 3:30 but the rest of the week, he or she starts at 9:30 and finish at 5:30.

- **Telecommuting.** This is an arrangement where staff may work part or all of their day/week at home. The value of this should be obvious, especially for those who have a lengthy commute to work each day. If they are able to eliminate two or three days of travel into the office or workplace, it has tremendous financial and work/life balance benefits for the staff member and, in fact, benefits society as rush hour sees fewer cars, fewer travellers, less pollution, etc. One of the often overlooked concerns in this particular approach is that the employer, in some jurisdictions, for the purposes of Occupational and Safety legislation, may be seen to have established another worksite and they are now responsible for safety in that worksite. Is the employee's office at home conducive to safe and healthy work practices? Is the home properly wired, heated, and ventilated? Are there safety hazards evident? If there are toys left on the stairs and the employee trips on them and breaks his or her back so he or she can't work anymore, where does the fault lie? What will the employer's obligation be? I believe there are ways of addressing these concerns, and they are not raised in an effort to deter creative arrangements but rather to encourage those considering telecommuting to be aware of all potential issues before jumping in. In many roles of mine over the years, I have enjoyed the benefits of working from home for part of my work week. It has proven, in those cases, to be beneficial for me, and in every instance the work of my employer was not only done but done with excellence. This can be a good and productive arrangement.
- **Time in lieu.** This arrangement, contained in many collective agreements, simply allows an employee the opportunity to bank some overtime hours or callback hours to be used at a

more convenient time for the employee instead of simply being paid outright for such overtime. There are usually limits placed on the bank in terms of the total number hours that can be banked, time limits within which they must be taken, how they can be scheduled, etc. For both employers and employees, it may help smooth out peaks and valleys in workload such that hours are accumulated during a particularly busy season and taken as time off when things are quieter.

- **Job sharing**. I remember being with one employer at a time when job sharing was a brand-new concept and hearing how "there is no way this can work." That was in 1985, and although job sharing doesn't exactly dominate the landscape for most employers, it continues to be requested by many staff to address their needs at a point in their lives when they are wanting more time off, usually to be with their kids or to gear down in readiness for retirement. The arrangement is simply one where one full-time job is shared between two job sharing partners. A schedule is drawn up to split the hours in some acceptable fashion (e.g., Person A works Monday, Tuesday, and Wednesday morning, while his partner works Wednesday afternoon, Thursday, and Friday. Another alternative might be that Person A works Monday and Tuesday this week but Wednesday, Thursday, and Friday next week, with his partner being available on the alternate days). Benefits may be split in any number of ways, and statutory holiday pay can also be split in a variety of fashions. Sick leave and vacation coverage need to be agreed to before commencing down this road. For job sharing to work, the partners must work effectively as a team and communicate with one another well and with their manager.

- **Compressed work weeks.** In this arrangement, an employee can work more than the usual daily hours in exchange for agreed-upon time off later in the schedule. For example, if a normal schedule involves five 8-hour workdays for a total work week of 40 hours, a compressed workweek may see an employee work four 10-hour days instead. Another variation might see them work three 12-hour days and a 36-hour paid workweek. It could also be something as simple as staff taking a half-hour lunch period instead of one hour in exchange for an extra day off every three weeks. Don't worry that the math may not add up for this example, as it is for illustrative purposes only. Many emergency personnel have been working compressed work weeks for years. There have been schedules set up that provide for 10-hour days, 12-hour days, and even some firefighters are now pushing for 24-hour shifts. In all cases, the employees want more time at home or perhaps better quality time for themselves. Benefits for employers (outside the usual benefits already addressed by having happier, less stressful employees) include things like reduced start up and shut down costs associated with production lines, report time is reduced, or there may be an opportunity to see increased hours for customer service.

- **Sabbatical leaves of absence.** In Ontario hospitals approximately 25 years ago, an agreement was reached to allow staff to work four years at 80 percent of their pay in exchange for having year five off to attend school or travel or whatever and continuing to receive 80 percent of their pay. Those of us in the field at the time worried that there would follow a groundswell of staff wanting to take advantage of our kindness in this regard. How would we ever be able to manage if more than a handful decided they wanted to go down this road? The fact that universities and colleges have been doing this for years didn't seem to enter our minds at the time. Needless to say, it worked. There was some uptake in the program, but it was not significant. For those who take advantage, it seems to be a great opportunity to do something with their lives that may not otherwise be possible. Scheduling for coverage of the absent employee may be a bit of a challenge in the fifth year, but so what? There are tax and benefits implications that need to be worked out ahead of time. Just make sure, as an employer, you are aware of all those implications ahead of time. As noted, it can be a wonderful opportunity for your staff or, who knows, even for yourself.

There are other life situations that may warrant different types of leaves. When I first started in the workforce, women who were pregnant had no right to maternity leave. They were simply required to quit their jobs and take their chances on getting it back when they were ready to return to work. That was then, and fortunately, major legislative changes have occurred to improve maternity leave benefits, in addition to paternity leave opportunities. But it doesn't need to end there. There are also parental leaves for most contemporary employers, as well as leaves for a host of other employee wants and needs from educational leaves to personal leaves to attend to ailing family members to leaves for purposes of travel or even to help avoid temporary layoffs or temporary downsizing.

Again, I suggest that you be open to any and all possibilities in this regard. Just be sure to have a full and complete understanding of all compensation and benefits arrangements ahead of time as well as a complete agreement on how long the leave will last, return to work dates, etc.

Some employers who feel compelled to give back to their communities as a sort of corporate social responsibility may also allow or even encourage employees to take paid time off work to volunteer for the employer's charity of choice. In some cases, employees are granted significant time off in order to lend their expertise to charities in the community. This is an arrangement that gives employees some new challenges, adds to their personal resume, helps the charity, and benefits the community.

Finally, some employers allow time off for employees to reduce working hours or their workload in order to prepare for retirement. This is easier for many people and is preferred to the alternative of working long, full-time hours for 40 years and then hitting retirement rather abruptly. The phasing in will also allow for a replacement employee to be completely and properly trained and orientated or may assist with any planned restructurings or work redistribution.

Work Arrangement Considerations

There are additional factors that need to be taken into consideration before blindly charging ahead with a new program or policy. Some of those issues include the following:

- There may be some initial start-up costs or administrative duties or time. For a telecommuting program, the computer systems of staff may need to linked to the workplace, and therefore there may be some minor costs associated with it. Additional leave programs may be nice in principle, but if staff need to be replaced with others on overtime, there may be some unanticipated costs. Think everything through before going forward.
- If there is a need for regular meetings, a schedule of communications, or even training programs that all staff need to be part of, make sure that the details are worked out in advance.
- Address issues of workload management or measurement.
- If customers are potentially affected by new work arrangements, ensure that their needs and demands will continue to be met.
- If the employee is to be absent from the workplace (for instance, working from home) make sure all staff know what the situation is and what the expectations of that employee are. Be transparent throughout.
- Make sure that any benefit program changes are adequately addressed ahead of time. If a full-time employee is to go on a

leave of absence or convert to part time for a period of time, what will the impact be on benefits? Will they need to be pro-rated? Are there any other conditions imposed by the benefits carrier?

- Be prepared for possible fallout from other staff. Not every member of your department will be as innovative as you or the staff member involved. You may hear grumbling from others about things like any perceived preferential treatment. That shouldn't stop you but be prepared.

I want to share a bit of a cautionary note at this point if you are dealing with unions, because they present a specific set of considerations. Unions are often reluctant to buy into the new order of things. They have a long history of pushing hard to get permanent full-time, well-paying jobs for all their members. We must respect that. However, for unions, the same message must be conveyed as the message to managers. The workforce is different today than it was 50 years ago, and so they too must now awaken to the new order of things. Their members must speak up. Not everybody in today's world wants full-time employment. Not everybody wants to show up at the workplace (wherever that may be) five days a week if they can be just as productive working from home or from some other satellite facility. We need to become more flexible.

Now, I know there are union representatives out there who are ready to slam me because they know of managers who will take advantage of this flexibility to force staff to become part time or increase the use of temporary or contract employees. To that claim I say "you're right." However, I'm also quick to point out that the change in attitude must come from all corners of the work world. Managers must improve their ability to help their staff, to treat them respectfully, to empathize with their home challenges, and to become much more flexible in the design of their work. We need to worry more about results and less about the hows and the wherefores.

Unions, for their part, need to see staff as individuals with unique needs and concerns. They don't all want to be regular, full-time staff throughout their entire careers. There may be times in their lives when they want to be home more often. Their union needs to respect these differences and work with the employer to accommodate all parties.

When considering alternative work arrangements, keep an open mind and remember our obligation as servant leaders to make those around us better. One way we can do this and contribute to a healthier, happier, more stress-free workforce is to consider new and different means of organizing our work, our schedules, and our lives. It is in everyone's best interests to be creative in this regard, but remember to dot all the *i*s and cross all the *t*s before going forward. It's worth it in the long run.

Key Messages
Alternative Work Arrangements

The only thing I can say about alternative work arrangements for any contemporary manager in any industry is "Try it." What's the worst thing that can happen? It's just like eating your peas and carrots.

1. Make sure you consider and understand the needs of your staff and the challenges they may face. They aren't all from the same generation or the same race, creed, colour, or background.
2. Be flexible with staff scheduling and work arrangements. Be creative at every chance you get.
3. Trust yourself and your staff and make sure they can trust you and each other.

Chapter 13:

Concluding Remarks

I started this publication with a view toward giving credit to mothers and fathers and caregivers everywhere for what they conveyed to us when we were young and the value that those messages continue to bring us each and every day. As we were growing up, our parents were the ones (and now that role belongs to next generations) who taught us life's lessons, which, for the most part, we carried forward with us into the workplace and ultimately formed the basis for many of the approaches we use in our management and leadership practices.

In addition to learning from our parents, I believe the time is long overdue for many managers to consider a paradigm shift from an approach that I would characterize as "command and control" to one that is more transparent and compassionate. I have served in management and leadership roles for close to 40 years and, every time things get difficult, we immediately look to cut expenses and the easiest target is to cut staff.

At the same time, we must look to reduce the education and training budget, increase productivity, and increase workload for those left behind. All of these pressures come on the backs of the staff that we so desperately need in order to achieve our organizational goals. Too often, they are still seen as just human resources that can be used and abused at will.

Why not, alternatively, treat them with kindness, compassion, and sensitivity, with the result being that we build a stronger team and enjoy better overall relations? Surely, this approach represents a better way. For all the years that I spent in the field of labour relations, expected to be a fighter for the employer, I thought that improvements could easily be made. The adversarial nature of labour relations is neither productive nor conducive to positive employment relations.

Throughout this book, I hope I have encouraged managers to begin to look at their role as involving something more than planning, organizing, implementing, delegating, controlling, and measuring. I hope that we can look at our work, like Theory Y, as being as natural as play. A job is something we need in order to pay the bills. Work, if it is as natural as play, is something that should be fun. As a result, after reading this book, there are a number of things I want you to start working hard at. I want you to do the following:

- Enjoy a positive work/life balance. Remember not to drop the ball that represents your family and those things that are truly important to you.
- Have fun at work. It's not just a job, and if it ever becomes that, it is time to reconsider your career choice.
- Always be nice, be polite, and be thankful for your friends, your family, your health, and the place we call home.
- Always do the right thing at the right time for the right reason. There is never a time or a reason to set aside ethics for any other good.
- Understand that conflict happens. It isn't always a bad thing. Deal with it and get on with it.

- Fulfill one of your most important roles as manager by being an effective coach and mentor for your staff. Our role as leader includes responsibility as an educator and ultimately to make our staff better as employees, as people, and as members of the community.
- Anticipate and learn to deal with change. It will always be with us. It always has been. Your staff may need help understanding and dealing with change. Be there for them.
- Conduct yourself as a true servant leader. I don't care if you label yourself as such, but remember how to behave. Help your staff to become better by serving them in any way you can.
- Grow your emotional intelligence. You can't do much about your IQ, but your EQ is learnable, and most assuredly it can be developed.
- Open your mind to new ways and means of organizing your workplace. It is a brave new world before us. Approach your life and your role with an attitude of optimism and a keen spirit of adventure and enthusiasm. Your staff will appreciate it and your organization will definitely be the key benefactor of your new approach.

Finally, *Common Sense Leadership* opened with a story about a field of daffodils. I feel it is appropriate to close this book with the same story. Remember the essential message: you can change your approach to the way you manage and lead, but it may only be possible one daffodil at a time. By sharing this story now, you will understand what I mean.

Several times my daughter had telephoned to say, "Mother, you must come to see the daffodils before they are over." It was a two-hour drive for me, and being cold and rainy, the prospect of seeing daffodils was not that exciting, especially when I was welcomed by the joyful sounds of my grandchildren, so happy to see me. In spite of my protests, my daughter insisted that we go and finally said, "You will never forgive yourself if we miss this experience." Away we went.

After about 20 minutes, we turned onto a small gravel road and I saw a small church. On the far side of the church, I saw a hand-lettered sign with an arrow that read, "Daffodil Garden." We got out of the car, each took a child's hand, and I followed Carolyn down the path. Then, as we turned a corner, I looked up and gasped. Before me lay the most glorious sight. It looked as though someone had taken a great vat of gold and poured it over the mountain and its surrounding slopes. The flowers were planted in majestic, swirling patterns, great ribbons, and swaths of deep orange, creamy white, lemon yellow, salmon pink, saffron, and butter yellow. Each different coloured variety was planted in large groups so that it swirled and flowed like its own river, with its own unique hue. There were five acres of flowers.

"Who did this?" I asked Carolyn.

"Just one woman," Carolyn answered. "She lives on the property. That's her home."

Carolyn pointed to a well-kept, small A-frame house sitting modestly in the midst of all that glory. We walked up to the house. On the patio, we saw a poster. "Answers to the questions I know you are asking" was the headline. The first answer was a simple one: "50,000 bulbs," it read. The second answer was "One at a time, by one woman. Two hands, two feet, and one brain." The third answer was "Began in 1958."

For me, that was a life-changing experience. I thought of this woman whom I had never met, who, almost 50 years earlier, had begun, one bulb at a time, to bring her vision of beauty and joy to an obscure mountaintop. Planting one bulb at a time, year after year, this unknown woman had forever changed the world in which she lived. One day at a time, she had created something of extraordinary magnificence, beauty, and inspiration. The principle that her daffodil garden taught is one of the greatest principles of celebration. That is, learning to move toward our goals and desires, one step at a time, often just one baby step at a time and learning to love the doing, learning to use the accumulation of time. When we multiply tiny pieces of time with small increments of daily effort, we, too, will find we can accomplish magnificent things. We can change the world.

The secret is to start now. It's so pointless to think of the lost hours of yesterdays. The way to make learning a lesson of celebration instead of a cause for regret is only to ask, "How can I put this to use today?"

The story is from an anonymous source, but its message is profound.

Good luck and best wishes.

Notes

1. Johns, Garth S., *Common Sense Leadership* (Ajax: Modern Media Perspectives, Canada, 2009), 9.
2. Ron Knowles, *Coming to Our Senses* (New York: Forbes Custom Publishing, 1999), 5.
3. Dan Carter, *Right Time Now* (Ajax: Modern Media Perspectives, Canada, 2006), 157.
4. James A. Autry, *The Servant Leader* (New York: Three Rivers Press, 2001), 8.
5. Lance Secretan, *The Spark, the Flame, and the Torch* (Caledon: The Secretan Centre, 2010), 113.
6. Graham Lowe, *Creating Healthy Organizations* (Toronto: University of Toronto Press, 2010), 30.
7. Stein, Steven J., and Howard E. Book, *The EQ Edge* (Mississauga: John Wiley and Sons, 2006), 14.
8. Travis Bradberry and Jean Greaves, *Emotional Intelligence 2.0* (San Diego: TalentSmart, 2009), 18–19.
9. Bradberry and Greaves, 14.
10. Dr. Linda Duxbury, Dr. Christopher Higgins, and Donna Coghill, Voices of Canadians (Human Resources Development Canada, 2003).
11. Jim Collins and Jerry I. Porras, *Built to Last* (New York: HarperCollins Publishers, 2002), 135–136.
12. Scott Adams, *This Is the Part Where You Pretend to Add Value* (Kansas City: Andrews McMeel Publishing, 2008).

13. Red Green, *How to Do Everything from the Man Who Should Know* (Toronto: DoubleDay Canada, 2010), 55.

14. Collins and Porras, *Built to Last*, 11.

15. Patrick Lencioni, *Silos, Politics, and Turf Wars* (San Francisco: Josey-Bass Publishing, 2006), 175.

16. General Rick Hillier, *Leadership* (New York: HarperCollins Publishers, 2010), 54.

17. Lencioni, *Silos, Politics, and Turf Wars*, 177.

18. Christine Pearson and Christine Porath, *The Cost of Bad Behaviour* (New York: The Penguin Group, 2009), 71–72.

19. Lowe, *Creating Healthy Organizations*, 104.

20. Thomas J. Peters and Robert H. Waterman Jr. *In Search of Excellence* (New York: Harper and Row Publishers, 1982).

21. Hillier, *Leadership*, 313.

22. Rosamund Stone Zander and Benjamin Zander, *The Art of Possibility* (New York: Penguin Books, 2000), 80.

23. Hillier, *Leadership*, 80–81.

24. Kevin Freiberg and Jackie Freiberg, *NUTS* (New York: Broadway Books, 1998), 213.

25. Robert I. Sutton, *The No Asshole Rule* (New York: Business Plus, 2007), 10.

26. Sutton, *The No Asshole Rule*, 46.

27. Gary T. Furlong, *The Conflict Resolution Toolbox* (Mississauga: John Wiley and Sons, 2005).

28. Spencer Johnson, *Who Moved My Cheese?* (New York: G. P. Putnam's Sons, 1998).

29. Thomas G. Crane, *The Heart of Coaching* (San Diego: FTA Press, 2007).

30. Duxbury et al., *Voices of Canadians*, 74.

Open Book Editions
A Berrett-Koehler Partner

Open Book Editions is a joint venture between Berrett-Koehler Publishers and Author Solutions, the market leader in self-publishing. There are many more aspiring authors who share Berrett-Koehler's mission than we can sustainably publish. To serve these authors, Open Book Editions offers a comprehensive self-publishing opportunity.

A Shared Mission

Open Book Editions welcomes authors who share the Berrett-Koehler mission—Creating a World That Works for All. We believe that to truly create a better world, action is needed at all levels—individual, organizational, and societal. At the individual level, our publications help people align their lives with their values and with their aspirations for a better world. At the organizational level, we promote progressive leadership and management practices, socially responsible approaches to business, and humane and effective organizations. At the societal level, we publish content that advances social and economic justice, shared prosperity, sustainability, and new solutions to national and global issues.

Open Book Editions represents a new way to further the BK mission and expand our community. We look forward to helping more authors challenge conventional thinking, introduce new ideas, and foster positive change.

For more information, see the Open Book Editions website: http://www.iuniverse.com/Packages/OpenBookEditions.aspx

Join the BK Community! See exclusive author videos, join discussion groups, find out about upcoming events, read author blogs, and much more! http://bkcommunity.com/